TREASURES
from the
Greek New Testament

WORD STUDIES IN
THE GREEK NEW TESTAMENT
For the English Reader

by Kenneth S. Wuest

1. GOLDEN NUGGETS FROM THE GREEK N. T.
2. BYPATHS IN THE GREEK N. T.
3. TREASURES FROM THE GREEK N. T.
4. UNTRANSLATABLE RICHES
5. PHILIPPIANS
6. FIRST PETER
7. GALATIANS
8. STUDIES IN VOCABULARY
9. HEBREWS
10. MARK
11. GREAT TRUTHS TO LIVE BY
12. THE PASTORAL EPISTLES
13. EPHESIANS AND COLOSSIANS
14. IN THESE LAST DAYS
15. PROPHETIC LIGHT IN THE PRESENT DARKNESS
16. ROMANS

THE NEW TESTAMENT IN EXPANDED TRANSLATION

TREASURES
from the
Greek New Testament
FOR THE ENGLISH READER

by

Kenneth S. Wuest
Moody Bible Institute

WM. B. EERDMANS PUBLISHING CO.
Grand Rapids   **Michigan**

TREASURES FROM THE GREEK NEW TESTAMENT
FOR THE ENGLISH READER
by KENNETH S. WUEST

Copyright, 1941, *by*
Wm. B. Eerdmans Publishing Co.

Set up and printed, March 1941
Twelfth printing, May 1976

ISBN 0-8028-1243-0

PHOTOLITHOPRINTED BY EERDMANS PRINTING COMPANY
GRAND RAPIDS, MICHIGAN, UNITED STATES OF AMERICA

DEDICATED

*To My Students in Greek
at the
Moody Bible Institute —
Lovers of the Greek New Testament*

PREFACE

A. T. Robertson in his book, *The Minister and His Greek New Testament*, says with reference to certain translations of the New Testament which he mentions: "We shall have many more. They will all have special merit, and they will all fail to bring out all that is in the Greek. One needs to read these translations; the more the better. But when he has read them all, there will remain a large and rich untranslatable element that the preacher ought to know. . . . It is not possible to reproduce the delicate turns of thought, the nuances of language, in translation. The freshness of the strawberry cannot be preserved in any extract."

It is the purpose of this book to bring to the Bible student who does not have access to the Greek, some of the untranslatable richness of the greatest book in all the world, the Greek New Testament. We have called this small volume which follows *Golden Nuggets from the Greek New Testament for the English Reader*, and *Bypaths in the Greek New Testament for the English Reader*: *Treasures from the Greek New Testament for the English Reader*. It follows the plan of its predecessors in treating only those things which the student of the English Bible cannot obtain for himself, and in presenting that material in such a simple, non-technical way that the average Christian, even though he has had no formal training in Bible study, can easily follow the author's thought.

While the book can be read as a series of articles, it should also prove useful as a reference work when light from the Greek text is desired upon any verse commented upon in the book. For this, the "Index to Scripture References" will be helpful. Or, when one is looking for some fresh bit of truth for a message, the material from the Greek text will be found rich in suggestiveness.

The English words treated are from the Authorized Version. The author's justification in sometimes offering a fuller or a slightly different translation is found in the fact that no single translation is able to bring out all the delicate shades of meaning, all the expressions peculiar to the Greek language, and for the reason that the standard translations are held down to a minimum of words which would best express the thought of the Greek, and rightly so. Then there are a limited number of English words that have changed their meaning in the last three hundred years since the Authorized Version was made. Since the majority of Bible students still use this version, it is necessary to take care of these words.

But we must not allow these facts to disturb our confidence in and dependence upon our reliable translations. We are concerned here with minor details, not with the great outstanding doctrines and facts in God's Word. Most men have been saved and have grown in grace through faith in the Word in its translated form. The Holy Spirit owns and quickens the translated Word, and has always done so. Therefore, as we seek to bring out from the Greek text aspects of truth that the translations do not handle, let us thank God for these translations which He has given us, and receive with gratefulness any added light which the labors of Bible students have been able to gather from the Greek text.

K. S. W.

The Moody Bible Institute,
Chicago, Illinois.

CONTENTS

CHAPTER PAGE

   I. The Word "Grace" in the New Testament 15

  II. Christian Optimism and a Carefree Mind 20

 III. "Golden Nugget" Promises 25

 IV. Greek Grammar and the Deity of Jesus Christ.... 31

   V. Is Future Punishment Everlasting? 34

 VI. Hell, Hades, and Tartarus 44

 VII. The Christian's "Thanatopsis" 48

VIII. A Pauline Paradox and Its Solution 50

 IX. Paul the Scholar 53

  X. Pauline Tactfulness 55

 XI. Amalgamated Love 57

 XII. The Word "Visit" in the New Testament 61

XIII. Here and There in the New Testament 65

XIV. An Exposition of the Greek Text of Romans VI.. 79

 XV. How to Be Hungry 107

XVI. The Four-Fold Basis of Christian Unity 109

XVII. The Meaning of "Perfect" in the New
       Testament 113

XVIII. About Anointing 122

XIX. Two Kinds of Testings 126

TREASURES
from the
Greek New Testament

I.

The Word "GRACE" in the New Testament

ARCHBISHOP TRENCH in his *Synonyms of the New Testament* says of this word, "It is hardly too much to say that the Greek mind has in no word uttered itself and all that was at its heart more distinctly than in this." This was his comment regarding the word "grace" as it was used in the language of pagan Greece. In the case of the use of the same word in the Greek New Testament, we can repeat this Greek scholar's words, substituting the word "God" for the word "Greek." *It is hardly too much to say that the mind of God has in no word uttered itself and all that was in His heart more distinctly than in this.*

We will look first at the way the word was used in pagan Greece, Greece with its philosophy, its athletics, its poetry and drama, its wonderful architecture and statuary, its blue skies and rugged mountains, its love of the beautiful. The word itself is a beautiful word, *charis*. It is pronounced as follows: *ch* as in Scotch lo*ch,* or as in our word *ch*asm, *a* as in father, *i* as in pol*i*ce, and the *s* as in cer*i*se. The voice is stressed on the first syllable. The Christian poet wrote "Grace! 'tis a charming sound, Harmonious to the ear; Heav'n with the echo shall resound, And all the earth shall hear. Saved by grace alone! This is all my plea: Jesus died for all mankind, And Jesus died for me." But of the latter, the Greeks of the pre-Christian era knew nothing.

15

Charis referred first of all to "that property in a thing which causes it to give joy to the hearers or beholders of it. . . . After awhile it came to signify not necessarily the grace or beauty of a thing, as a quality appertaining to it; but the gracious or beautiful thing, act, thought, speech, or person it might be, itself — the grace embodying and uttering itself, where there was room or call for this, in gracious outcomings toward such as might be its objects . . . There is a further sense which the word obtained, namely, the thankfulness which the favor calls out in return. . . . In the ethical terminology of the Greek schools *charis* implied ever a favor freely done, without claim or expectation of return. . . . Thus Aristotle, defining *charis*, 'lays the whole stress on this very point, that it is conferred freely, with no expectation of return, and finding its only motive in the bounty and free-heartedness of the giver'."* Charis was also used to describe an act that was beyond the ordinary course of what might be expected, and was therefore commendable.

This word the inspired writers take over into the New Testament. In a few instances it has its distinctively classical meaning, but in the other places where it is used, it takes an infinite step forward to a deeper, richer, more wonderful content of meaning. Luke uses it in its purely classical meaning when he says (4:22), "And all bare him witness, and wondered at the gracious words which proceeded out of his mouth." Here the word has its classical meaning of that property in our Lord's words which caused them to give joy to the hearers. How wonderful it must have been to hear the Lord Jesus speak in human speech and human tones. Not only was the content of His words gracious and beautiful, but the tones of His voice must have reflected all the depth of His personality, the intensity of His convictions (John 2:17), the fervor of His desire to

---
*Trench

serve (Matt. 20:28), the pathos and tenderness of His sorrow (Matt. 23:37-39). It was the infinite God speaking with human lips and in human tones.

Both Luke (17:9) and Paul in Romans 6:17 and II Corinthians 8:16 use *charis* in its classical meaning of "thankfulness." Peter uses the word in its meaning of "that which is beyond the ordinary course of what might be expected, and is therefore commendable," in his first epistle (2:19, 20), where the words "thankworthy" and "acceptable" are the translations of *charis* which appears in the Greek text. Surely, for a slave to manifest a spirit of patient submission toward a master who mistreats him, is an action beyond the ordinary course of what might be expected and is therefore commendable. The usual reaction on the part of a slave who is mistreated is to rebel against his master.

But how this purely classical meaning of the word describes what took place at Calvary. All the human race could expect in view of its sin, was the righteous wrath of a holy God, that and eternal banishment from His glorious presence. But instead, that holy God stepped down from His judgment seat and took upon Himself at Calvary's Cross, the guilt and penalty of human sin, thus satisfying His justice and making possible the bestowal of His mercy. And this He did, not for those who were His friends, but His bitter enemies, unlovely creatures saturated with sin. *Charis* in classical Greek referred to a favor conferred freely, with no expectation of return, and finding its only motive in the bounty and free-heartedness of the giver. This favor was always done to a friend, never to an enemy. Right here *charis* leaps forward an infinite distance, for the Lord Jesus died for His enemies (Rom. 5:8-10), a thing unheard of in the human race. Surely this was beyond the ordinary course of what might be expected and is therefore commendable. This is what John is speaking of in his first epistle (3:1) when he says, "Behold, what manner of love the Father has bestowed on us, that we should be called the children of God." The words "what manner of" are from a Greek word which means "what foreign kind of." That is, the love shown by God at the Cross is foreign to the human race. Man simply does not act that way (Rom. 5:7, 8, 10). That is why God's action at the Cross in dying for lost humanity is an action beyond the ordinary course of what might be expected and is therefore commendable. Here is one of the strongest proofs of the divine source of the Bible. The substitutionary atonement never came from the philosophies of man but from the heart of God.

Thus, the word *charis* comes to its highest and most exalted content of meaning in the New Testament. It refers to God's offer of salvation with all that that implies, which salvation was procured at Calvary's Cross with all the personal sacrifice which that included, offered to one who is His bitter enemy and who is not only undeserving of that salvation but deserves condign punishment for his sins, offered without any expectation of return, but given out of the bounty and free-heartedness of the giver. This means that there is no room for good works on the part of the sinner as a means whereby he could earn his salvation, or after salvation whereby he might retain that salvation. Paul sets grace over against works as things directly in opposition to one another so far as the means of salvation is concerned (Rom. 4:4-5, 11:6). But Paul is very careful to make plain that good works naturally issue from and are required by grace (Titus 2:11-12).

Furthermore, he shows that this grace is unlimited in its resources. In Romans 5:20 he says, "Where sin abounded, grace did much more abound." The word "abound" is from a different Greek word than that which is translated "abounded." It is a compound word made up of a verb which means "to exist in superabundance," and a prefixed preposition which means "above." The translation could read "grace existed in superabundance and then more grace added to this superabundance."

Thus, salvation is a gift, to be received by the open hand of faith, not something to be earned. Dear reader, if you have been attempting to find acceptance with God by your good works, if you have been depending in the least upon any personal merit, will you not now cast aside all this, and accept the free grace of God by faith in Jesus Christ as your personal Saviour, the One who died on the Cross for you, pouring out His precious blood as the God-appointed sacrifice for sins? "For God so loved the world that He gave His Son, the only begotten One, that whosoever believeth in Him might not perish but have everlasting life" (John 3:16).

II.

Christian Optimism and a Carefree Mind

"BLESSED be the God and Father of our Lord Jesus Christ, which according to his abundant mercy hath begotten us again unto a lively hope by the resurrection of Jesus Christ from the dead. . . . Wherefore gird up the loins of your mind, be sober, and hope to the end for the grace that is to be brought unto you at the revelation of Jesus Christ" (I Peter 1:3, 13).

The English word "blessed" is the translation of two totally different Greek words in the New Testament. In Matthew 5:1-12 it is the rendering of a Greek word which means "prosperous." Here the context limits its meaning to spiritual prosperity. That is, "spiritually prosperous are the poor in spirit: for theirs is the kingdom of heaven." Heaven's blessings flood the soul of those saints who have a contrite and humble heart. Their prosperity consists of heaven's blessings. Their spiritual condition is prosperous. The word "blessed" in the text under consideration is from a Greek word which means "to speak well of." The word comes into our language in the words "eulogy" and "eulogize." The idea is that of "praising." However, there is another word in Greek which means "praise." We could translate, "Let the God and Father of our Lord Jesus Christ be well spoken of."

The words "according to" are from a Greek word which literally means "down." The idea is not "according to the measure or extent of His mercy," but "impelled by His mercy." God's merciful heart impelled Him to do what He did at the Cross, die for a race of lost sinners. We were begotten again, the translation tells us. The word "again" is from a Greek word which has two meanings, "again," and "from above," the meaning to be used being determined by the context. Our Lord in John 3:3 uses it in its meaning "again," since Nicodemus understands Him to speak of a second birth as he says, "How can a man be born when he is old? can he enter the second time into his mother's womb, and be born?" There are two words in Greek meaning "again," one refers to the mere repetition of an action, the other, to the repetition of an action, the repeated action having the same source as the first act. The latter is used here. The second birth has its source in the Spirit. The first act was the impartation of divine life to Adam.

One result of being born from above is that the believer has a lively hope. The word "lively" is from the Greek word which speaks of the life principle. It is the word used when the inspired writers speak of eternal life. The word "lively" in the Greek text is not an adjective but a participle. A participle is a verbal adjective, having the action of a verb and the descriptive powers of an adjective. The word "hope" is described by an action. The word "lively" is an excellent translation. The margin gives "living." But it is more than a hope that is alive. It is actively alive. This hope is an energizing principle, a spontaneous, overflowing, buoyant thing. It is a hopefulness, a spirit of optimism, a looking ever upon the bright side of things, a looking forward to only that which is good, an expectancy of continued blessing and joy. It is the opposite of that fear of the future which grips so many hearts. This Christian optimism, this exuberant hopefulness, leaves no room for worry. This lively hope should be the normal atmosphere of every Christian heart.

How may we have it? By yielding to the One whose ministry it is to produce this hopefulness in our hearts, the Holy Spirit. This Christian optimism is a heaven-born thing, something supernatural. The secret of enjoying it is in the fullness of the Holy Spirit. The secret of the fullness of the Spirit is in a moment by moment desire for that fullness, and a moment by moment trust in the Lord Jesus for the same (John 7:37, 38). And so Peter says, "Praised be the God and Father of our Lord Jesus Christ who, impelled by His great mercy, begot us from above, so that we have a spontaneous, buoyant, exultant spirit of hopefulness, this begetting having been accomplished through the intermediate instrumentality of the resurrection of Jesus Christ out from among those who are dead."

In connection with and in view of this Christian optimism, Peter exhorts us to have a carefree mind. He says, "Gird up the loins of your mind." The words "gird up" are from a construction in the Greek which is literally, "having girded up," the God-expected duty of every saint. We have here an oriental expression which must be explained. The people to whom Peter addressed this letter wore long, flowing, loose, outer garments. Preparatory to engaging in physical exertion such as running, they would gather these garments about their loins so that they would not impede the free action of the limbs. Peter tells us that we are pilgrims on our way home to heaven, and as such, must ever be ready to be on the move, that is, in a spiritual sense. The exhortation therefore is to put out of the way all that disturbs our minds, things that would impede the free exercise of our spiritual faculties. We know how worry, fretfulness, fear, anger, and their related mental attitudes

all freeze up the mind and make it unfit for the best kind
of work and the highest type of Christian life. In view of
the fact that the Holy Spirit is producing in the Christian's
heart that buoyant spirit of hopefulness, it is the responsibility of that Christian to put out of his mind everything
that would disturb that Christian optimism which always
hopes for the best and always looks on the bright side of
things. The believer can do that by the same power of the
Holy Spirit which produces this lively hope. This is what
we mean by a carefree mind.

It is not a mind which does not recognize the respon-
sibilities of life, but a mind free from care, for Peter says,
"Wherefore, having put out of the way all that disturbs
your mind (thus allowing that buoyant Christian hopefulness to predominate), being mentally self-controlled and
calm, set your hope perfectly, wholly, unchangeably, and
without doubt and despondency upon the grace which is
being brought to you upon the occasion of the revelation
of Jesus Christ." The words "be sober" in our translation
refer to a mental self-control and calmness. The words
"hope to the end" do not refer to the length of time this
hope is held, but to the quality of this hope, a hope that is
a perfect, unchangeable one. The hope in verse three is
a subjective one, being an inner hopefulness, the normal
Christian attitude towards life, whereas the hope of verse
thirteen is an objective hope, resting itself upon some future happening, here the glorification of the believer at the
return of the Lord into the air. This is the grace which is
being brought to the believer. The word "brought" is not
future in the Greek, but present. Our glorification is not
looked upon as a future event which is isolated from the
two other parts of our salvation, namely, our justification
and our sanctification. It is part of our salvation. It is on
the Divine Menu. When we sit down to a sumptuous re-

past, we are never concerned as to whether there will be dessert or not. We know it is on the menu. So why be in doubt as to whether you as a true believer in the Lord Jesus as your personal Saviour, will reach heaven and all that goes with the glories of that blessed place? It is all on the Divine Menu placed before us in God's holy Word.

The normal Christian life lived in the fullness of the Holy Spirit is a life in which a supernaturally produced Christian optimism and a carefreeness of mind make possible the most efficient use of our spiritual faculties, used to the glory of God. Do not allow Satan to rob you of this precious heritage.

III.

"Golden Nugget" Promises

THE first one is, "He hath said, 'I will never leave thee, nor forsake thee'" (Heb. 13:5). The translation says, "He hath said." But it is intensive in the Greek. "He Himself hath said." That is, the Lord Jesus Himself personally made this promise. The word "leave" is not from the usual Greek word which means "to leave," but from a word which means "to uphold" or "sustain." In the Greek there are two negatives before the word "leave," presenting a very strong negation. The promise is, "I will not, I will not cease to uphold or sustain thee." Thus Paul can say "I am strong for all things through the One who infuses strength in me" (Phil. 4:13). We are assured therefore of the sustaining grace of God as we go through trials and testing times.

The word "forsake" is a composite of three words, "to leave," "down," and "in." The first has the idea of forsaking one. The second suggests rejection, defeat, helplessness. The third refers to some place or circumstance in which a person may find himself helpless, forsaken. The meaning of the word is that of forsaking someone in a state of defeat or helplessness in the midst of hostile circumstances. The word means in its totality, "to abandon, to desert, to leave in straits, to leave helpless, to leave destitute, to leave in the lurch, to let one down." There are three negatives before this word, making the promise one of triple assurance. It

is, "I will not, I will not, I will not forsake thee." Not only
do we have the assurance of God's all-sufficient sustaining
power to hold us true to Him and in perfect peace as we go
through testing times, but we have His promise that He will
never abandon us, never desert us, never leave us in straits
but will come to our help, never leave us destitute but will
supply all our need, never leave us in the lurch but will see
to it that we are rescued from the difficulties in which we
sometimes find ourselves. *He will never let us down.*

The second promise is, "Him that cometh to me I will
in no wise cast out" (John 6:37). Here again we have two
negatives before the verb: "I will not, I will not cast out."
The words "cast out" are from one word made up of two
words, the word "to throw" and a preposition meaning
"out from within." That is, our Lord is speaking of those
who are in salvation, in the Father's house. He gives us a
double-strength promise that He will not throw us out of
that house. But there is another word in the Greek which
does not appear in the English, the word "outside." Literally, the promise reads, "The one who comes to Me, I will
not, I will not throw out into the outside." Imagine a heavenly Father throwing His own child out. That is exactly
what the Greek word means. This word "outside" is found
in Revelation 22:15, where it is translated "without." The
New Jerusalem is spoken of in the previous verse, but
"without," that is, "outside, are dogs, and sorcerers, and
whoremongers, and murderers, and idolaters, and whosoever loveth and maketh a lie." We have the solemn promise
of our Lord that the Christian will never be ejected from
the Father's house and thrown into the outside where
those are who have rejected His grace.

The third is, "If ye abide in me, and my words abide in
you" (John 15:7). The words, "ye shall ask," are in the
you, ye shall ask what ye will, and it shall be done unto

imperative mood, which makes them a command, and are to be taken in the sense of "I command you to ask." "Abiding" implies fellowship with the Lord, "nothing between myself and my Saviour," and dependence upon Him. To those who thus abide, God issues the gracious command, "ask whatever ye desire." It is more than a command. It is a challenge. It is as if God said, "You meet the conditions, and I challenge you to ask, and then see how faithful and able I am to answer your prayer." The word "desire" implies a desire that proceeds, not from deliberate forethought, but from inclination. This is a perfectly safe command and promise, because when we live in close fellowship with Jesus, our desires and our inclinations are His desires and His inclinations. The word "ask" is in the middle voice which speaks of the subject of the verb acting in its own interest. Therefore we translate, "ask for yourselves." But as we live in intimate fellowship with Jesus, those things which we ask for ourselves, we ask, not for the purpose of gratifying a selfish desire, but for the purpose of glorifying Him. Prayers of that kind are answered.

The word "done" is not from the Greek word which means to do something in the sense of making something. That would imply taking something in existence and fashioning it to suit our needs. The word is from the Greek word meaning "to become, to come into existence." God will if necessary bring into existence that for which we asked. The word "ask" is in the aorist tense which when used in a command means, "do at once what is commanded." Thus as we are abiding in Jesus, we are commanded not to hesitate, but to ask at once. The translation reads, "If ye abide in Me, and my words abide in you, I command you to ask at once and for yourselves whatever ye desire, and it shall be yours."

The fourth promise is, "My sheep hear my voice, and I know them, and they follow me, and I give unto them eternal life; and they shall never perish, neither shall any man pluck them out of my hand. My Father which gave them me, is greater than all; and no man is able to pluck them out of my Father's hand. I and my Father are one" (John 10:27-30). The expression, "they shall never perish" is a very strong one in the Greek. There are two negatives before the word "perish." "They shall not, they shall not perish." In addition to the double negative, there are three words which follow the word "perish," which are translated by the one word "never." The phrase is found in John 6:51, where it is translated "forever." The Greek papyri give an instance where the crowd in a public meeting cries repeatedly, "the emperors forever,"* using the Greek phrase found in this verse. The noun in the phrase means "eternal," and has the same root as the adjective "eternal" in the words "eternal life" in verse 28. The English language creaks and groans in its effort to translate the Greek here. "They shall not, they shall not perish, no, not eternally." The word "eternal" gives an infinite reach to the two negatives.

The word "man" is in italics, which means that it is not in the Greek text, and is supplied by the translators to complete the sense. There are two words in the Greek language meaning "a man," but neither is used here. The word "any" is an indefinite pronoun in the Greek, and the word "one" would complete its meaning better than the word "man." The translation "anyone" is truer to the sense of the original. That includes Satan. The word "pluck" is literally "snatch," and is often used in a bad sense as when death snatches its victim or where someone carries something off by force. When we consider the size of God's hand,

*Moulton and Milligan.

large enough to hold all of the oceans on earth, wide enough to stretch from where the east begins and where the west ends (Isaiah 40:12), we can understand why no one, including Satan himself, is able to snatch the believer out of its protecting care.

The word "gave" in verse 29 is in the perfect tense in Greek, which tense refers to a past completed action having present results. The aorist tense is the customary tense to use in Greek when the writer merely wishes to speak of the fact of the action. Whenever a writer uses another tense, he goes out of his way to do so, which means that he has some special information to convey to the reader. The perfect tense here is like a carpenter who drives a nail through a board, and then to assure himself that it is there to stay, he clinches it on the other side. The Father gave believers to the Lord Jesus as a permanent gift to be retained permanently by Him. And then, not only are we in the clasp of the hand of our Lord, but we are safely resting in the hand of God the Father. Two hands of infinite proportions are holding us in salvation. And the owners of these hands are one in essence, two Persons of the Triune God.

The fifth promise is, "Whosoever drinketh of this water shall thirst again: but whosoever drinketh of the water that I shall give him shall never thirst; but the water that I shall give him shall be in him a well of water springing up into everlasting life" (John 4:13, 14).

The first occurrence of the word "drinketh" is in a construction in the Greek which refers to continuous action, and the second use of the word in the original presents the mere fact of the action without reference to the progress of the action. The fuller translation therefore reads, "Every one who keeps on constantly drinking of this water shall thirst again. But whosoever takes a drink of the water which I shall give him shall never thirst." The words "shall never thirst" are from a construction in the Greek in which there are two negatives before the verb, and a phrase which means "forever," which comes after the verb. The idea is, "shall not, shall not thirst, ever." A double negative in the Greek does not make a positive statement but only strengthens the negation. The word "forever" gives an infinite reach to the two negatives.

In the Greek text, John reports the Samaritan woman as speaking of a well of water, and our Lord as speaking of a spring of water, while both words are translated by the one English word "well." The person who keeps on drinking of the wells of the world, lifeless, dull, brackish, polluted, stale, will thirst again. The world with all its sin does not satisfy, never can. But the person who takes one drink of the spring of eternal life never thirsts again.

The reason why one drink satisfies is that when the sinner takes one drink of eternal life, that one drink becomes in him a spring of water leaping up into a fountain of eternal life. The word "be" is in the Greek literally "become," and the word "well" is from the Greek word meaning a "spring." The one drink is itself a spring that ever keeps bubbling up, ever refreshing and satisfying the one who takes a drink of the water of life. This spring becomes a river of living water (John 7:37, 38), and this living water is just a symbol of the indwelling Holy Spirit who constantly ministers the Lord Jesus to the believer. And because Jesus completely satisfies, the person who takes one drink of this living water, never thirsts again. Have you experienced the truth of this promise?

IV.

Greek Grammar and the Deity of Jesus Christ

THE New Testament in its English translation plainly teaches that Jesus Christ is the second Person of the Triune God, possessing the same essence as God the Father. It is interesting to know that a rule of Greek grammar brings out the same truth.

The rule is as follows: When two nouns in the same case are connected by the Greek word "and," and the first noun is preceded by the article "the," and the second noun is not preceded by the article, the second noun refers to the same person or thing to which the first noun refers, and is a farther description of it. For instance, the words "pastors" and "teachers" in Eph. 4:11 are in the same case and are connected by the word "and." The word "pastors," is preceded by the article "the," whereas the word "teachers" is not. This construction requires us to understand that the words "pastors" and "teachers" refer to the same individual, and that the word "teacher" is a farther description of the individual called a "pastor." The expression therefore refers to pastors who are also teachers, "teaching-pastors."

This rule also applies to the following passages where the names "God" and "Father" are in the same case and are connected by the Greek word "and," while the word "God" is preceded by the article, and the word "Father" is not. The Greek word "and" can be translated by any of the following words, "and, even, also," depending upon the context in which it is found. In the passages under discussion, it is translated by "and" or "even." These passages are Romans 15:6; I Corinthians 15:24; II Corinthians 1:3, 11:31; Galatians 1:4; Ephesians 5:20; Philippians 4:20; I Thessalonians 1:3, 3:11, 13, where God and the Father are not two persons but one and the same, and the word "Father" is a farther description of the Person called "God."

In II Peter 1:11, 2:20, and 3:18, we have the phrase, "Lord and Saviour Jesus Christ." Here we find the same construction in the Greek text. The same rule of grammar applies. The Lord and the Saviour are the same person, the word "Saviour" being a farther description of the Person described as "Lord." This speaks of the deity of Jesus Christ, because the Greek word translated "Lord" was used as a name of Deity. The translators of the Septuagint version of the Old Testament (285-150 B.C.) used it to translate the august title of God, "Jehovah." The word was used in the Roman empire as a name for the ruling Caesar who was worshipped as a god. Christianity challenged the imperialism of the Caesars by announcing that there was born "in the city of David a Saviour, which is Christ the Lord" (Luke 2:11). The word "Lord" was an accepted title of Deity in the terminology of Israel, the Roman empire, and Christianity. Thus, a simple rule of Greek grammar teaches the deity of Jesus Christ.

But to make the case still stronger, we find in II Peter 1:1 the expression, "God and our Saviour Jesus Christ," where the same construction occurs, and the same rule of grammar applies. Solid ground for correct translation and interpretation is found in a careful application of the rules of Greek grammar. The inspired writers of the New Testament held to the grammar of the international Greek spoken throughout the Roman world. Only in that way could they expect to be correctly understood. Thus Greek grammar testifies that Jesus Christ is Lord, the Jehovah of the Old Testament, and Deity, the God of the New Testament. The apostles uniformly testify that Jesus Christ is God, and this is just another example of their statements challenging the Imperial Cult of the Caesar. The translation should read, "through the righteousness of our God and Saviour, Jesus Christ." The Roman emperor was recognized by his subjects as their god and their saviour. Peter tells us that Jesus Christ is the God and the Saviour of Christians.

In Titus 2:13 we have "the great God and our Saviour Jesus Christ." We find the same construction in the Greek, and the same rule of grammar requires us to interpret the phrase as teaching that Jesus Christ is the great God. Since the Greek word for "and" should be translated by the word "even" where the context demands such a meaning, we are justified in rendering this phrase "the great God, even our Saviour Jesus Christ," for the grammatical construction demands that the two expressions, "the great God," and "Saviour Jesus Christ," refer to one individual. The word "even" brings out this meaning. The translation could also read, "our great God and Saviour, Jesus Christ." Thus the rules of Greek grammar teach the deity of Jesus Christ.

V.

Is Future Punishment Everlasting?

THE Church has always held tenaciously to the teaching
that the punishment of those who enter eternity unsaved, is unending. There is abundant evidence in the apoc-
ryphal literature of Israel to show that that nation believed
and taught the same thing. Of late, however, the assertion
is being made that this punishment is for a limited time
only, this contention being based upon the statement that
the two Greek words used to describe this punishment, refer to a limited period of time. These two words are, the
noun, *aion,* and the adjective, *aionios.*

We submit Moulton and Milligan in their *Vocabulary of
the Greek Testament* as our first authority. The work of
these scholars is recognized as the latest advance in New
Testament research, since it is based upon the study of the
Greek secular documents known as "The Papyri." These
latter are the last court of appeal on the usage of Greek
words in the first century. They give two uses for *aion.*
In a phrase from one of these early manuscripts, "For the
rest of your life," *aion* refers to a limited period of time. A
public meeting at Oxyrhynchus was punctuated with cries
of "The Emperors forever," where *aion* has the meaning
of "unending."

They have this to say about *aionios.* "Without pro-
nouncing any opinion on the special meaning which the-

ologians have found for this word, we must note that outside the New Testament, in the vernacular as well as in
classical Greek (see Grimm-Thayer), it never loses the sense
of *perpetuus*. It is a standing epithet of the emperor's
power." Webster's International Dictionary derives our
English word "perpetual," meaning "continuing forever,
everlasting, eternal, unceasing" (its own definition), from
this Latin word *perpetuus*. They give as an illustration of
the use of *aionios* the sentence, "I confess that I should
show myself grateful for your loving-kindness forever."
Their closing comment on *aionios* is, "In general, the word
depicts that of which the horizon is not in view, whether
the horizon be at an infinite distance, or whether it lies no
farther than the span of a Caesar's life."

Our next authority is *Biblico-Theological Lexicon of
New Testament Greek,* by Herman Cremer, D.D. He says
of *aion*: "In early Greek especially, and still also in Attic,
aion signifies the duration of human life as limited to a
certain space of time, hence the meanings, *the duration of
life, course of life, term of life, lifetime, life in its temporal
form.* From this original limitation of the conception to
human life, it may be explained how it sometimes denotes
the space of a human life, a human generation. Accordingly, the expansion of the conception of time unlimited was
easy, for it simply involved the abstraction of the idea of
limitation, and thus the word came to mean *unlimited duration.* Inasmuch, therefore, as *aion* may denote either the
duration of a definite space of time, or the (unending) duration of time in general, both future and past, according to
the context, it was the proper term for rendering the Hebrew *olam,*—for which the LXX (Greek translation of Old
Testament) used it constantly, the only distinction being
that the Hebrew word meant primarily, a remote, veiled,
undefined, and therefore, unlimited time, past or future,

and only secondarily, a definite (especially future) period
whose limits must be ascertained by the context."

As to *aionios*, Cremer has but these brief words: *"Aionios*
refers to time in its duration, constant, abiding, eternal."

We come now to the testimony of *A Greek-English Lexicon of the New Testament* by Joseph Henry Thayer, D.D.
He gives as the first meaning of *aion, age, a human lifetime,
life itself,* and for the second meaning, *an unbroken age,
perpetuity of time, eternity.* His meanings of *aionios* are,
first, *without beginning or end, that which has always been
and always will be,* second, *without beginning,* third, *without end, never to cease, everlasting.* When comparing the
synonyms, *aidios* and *aionios* he says, "*aidios* covers the
complete philosophical idea—without beginning and without end; *also* either without beginning *or* without end, as
respects the past; it is applied to what has existed *time out
of mind. Aionios* (from Plato on) gives prominence to the
immeasurableness of eternity (while such words as *sun-
eches, continuous, unintermitted, diateles, perpetual, lasting to the end,* are not so applicable to an abstract term,
like *aion*); *aionios* accordingly is especially adapted to
supersensuous things."

Finally, we quote Liddell and Scott in their *Greek-English Lexicon* (classical). *Aion* means *a space or period of
time, a lifetime, life, an age, generation, an indefinitely long
time, a space of time, eternity. Aionios* means *lasting, eternal.* Dr. E. B. Pusey* quotes J. Reddel, the best Greek Ox-
ford scholar of his day as stating that *aionios* in classical
Greek was used strictly of eternity, an eternal existence,
such as shall be, when time shall be no more.

These authorities agree on the two meanings of *aion,*
that of a limited space of time, and that of eternity, never

*What is of Faith as to Everlasting Punishment?

ending, everlasting, the meaning to be used in any particular instance to be determined by the context in which it is found. They also agree upon the meaning of *aionios,* that it refers to time in its duration, constant, abiding, eternal, continuing forever, everlasting.

Our next step will be to show that in certain passages in the New Testament where *aion* appears, it cannot be used in its meaning of "a limited space of time," but can only mean "eternal." These passages have to do with the being of the Son of God, His reign, His glory, His throne, His priesthood, His post-resurrection life, none of which is of limited duration, for everything about God is of infinite proportions. These are Luke 1:33, 55; John 8:35 (second occurrence), 12:34; Romans 1:25, 9:5, 11:36, 16:27; II Corinthians 11:31; Galatians 1:5; Ephesians 3:11; Philippians 4:20; I Timothy 1:17; II Timothy 4:18; Hebrews 1:8; 5:6, 6:20, 7:17, 21, 24, 28; 13:8, 21; I Peter 4:11, 5:11; II Peter 3:18; Revelation 1:6, 18, 4:9, 10, 5:13, 7:12, 10:6, 11:15, 15:7. Instances where *aionios* is used, and where it can only mean "eternal," because its context speaks of the being of God, the glory of God, and the covenant of blood are Romans 16:26; Hebrews 9:14; 13:20, I Peter 5:10. This establishes the fact that the New Testament usage of *aion* and *aionios* includes their meaning of "eternal," whatever other meanings the former might have in other contexts such as those of "a limited period of time" (Colossians 1:26), or "an age as characterized by a certain system of evil" (Romans 12:2). As to *aionios,* the only places in the New Testament where it is translated by any other words than "eternal" or "everlasting" are Romans 16:25, II Timothy 1:9, and Titus 1:2 where it is rendered by the word "world." But even here it refers to "that which is anterior to the most remote period in the past conceivable by any imagination that man knows of" (*Expositor's Greek Testament*), namely, to the eternity before time began as we know it, time which runs concurrently with the created universe and the affairs of the human race. Thus, both *aion* and *aionios* are used in the New Testament in their meanings of "everlasting" and "eternal."

Now we come to the passages in the New Testament where *aionios* is used in connection with the life God gives the believer when He saves him. We have seen that this word is used in connection with the being of God, and that it can only mean "eternal" in this case. But the life which God gives the believer is Christ (Col. 3:4), which means that *aionios* when it describes the life given the believer, must mean "eternal," which agrees with the uniform meaning given by the four Greek authorities quoted. In all its occurrences in the New Testament, *aionios* never refers to a limited extent of time, but always to that which is eternal or everlasting. Even in Romans 16:25, II Timothy 1:9, and Titus 1:2, it refers to the eternity before time began. For the benefit of the student who does not have access to a Greek concordance, we list the passages where *aionios* is used in connection with the life given the believer; Mark 10:17, 30; Luke 10:25, 18:18, 30; John 3:15, 16, 36, 4:14, 36, 5:24, 39, 6:27, 40, 47, 54, 68, 10:28, 12:25, 50, 17:2, 3; Acts 13:46, 48; Romans 2:7, 5:21, 6:22, 23; II Corinthians 4:17, 18; 5:1; Galatians 6:8; I Timothy 1:16, 6:12; II Timothy 2:10; Titus 1:2, 3:7; Hebrews 5:9, 9:12; I Peter 5:10; I John 1:2, 2:25, 3:15, 5:11, 13, 20; Jude 21.

This brings us to the places where *aion* is used in connection with this same life, and because this life is eternal, *aion* must mean "eternal" here, not "an age"; Mark 10:17; John 4:14, 6:51, 58, 8:51, 52, 10:28, 11:26.

We have found that the life God gives the believer is described by two words, *aion* and *aionios,* both meaning "eternal." We notice now the statement of our Lord in Matthew

25:46, "These shall go away into *(aionios)* everlasting punishment: but the righteous into life *(aionios)* eternal."
Aionios means "eternal" when used with the word "life."
Does it mean "eternal" when used with the word "punishment"?

But now we will let Dr. E. B. Pusey speak,* as he quotes
Augustine on this passage, and then adds his own comment.
Augustine said of this text, "What a thing it is, to account
eternal punishment to be a fire of long duration, and eternal life to be without end, since Christ comprised both in
that very same place, in one and the same sentence, saying, 'These shall go into eternal punishment, but the righteous into life eternal.' If both are eternal, either both
must be understood to be lasting with an end, or both perpetual without end. For like is related to like; on the one
side, eternal punishment; on the other side, eternal life.
But to say in one and the same sentence, life eternal shall
be without end, punishment eternal shall have an end,
were too absurd: whence, since the eternal life of the
saints shall be without end, punishment eternal too shall
doubtless have no end to those whose it shall be."

Dr. Pusey adds the following to Augustine's words: "The
argument is not merely from language. It has a moral and
religious aspect. Any ordinary writer who drew a contrast
between two things, would, if he wished to be understood,
use the self-same word in the self-same sense. He would
avoid ambiguity. If he did not, we should count him ignorant of language, or if it were intentional, dishonest. I
ask, 'In what matter of this world would you trust one who
in any matter of this world, should use the self-same word
in two distinct senses in the self-same sentence, without giving any hint that he was so doing?' In none. Find any case
in which you would trust a man who did so in the things of

What is of Faith as to Everlasting Punishment?

men, and then ascribe it to your God in the things of God. I could not trust man. I could not believe it of my God."

It remains for us to examine the New Testament passages where *aion* and *aionios* are used of the future punishment of the lost. We will look first at those passages which contain *aionios*. In Matthew 18:8 the phrase "everlasting fire" is in the Greek "the fire which is everlasting." The use of the definite article shows that this passage does not refer to fire in general but to a particular fire (Rev. 20:10). This fire will burn forever and is unquenchable (Mark 9:43). Matthew 25:41 tells us that this everlasting fire is prepared for the devil and his angels. The word "prepared" in the Greek is in the perfect tense, which tense speaks of a past complete action that has present results. The Lake of Fire had been prepared before our Lord spoke these words, and is now in existence. The fires of this lake are not purifying but punitive. That is, their purpose is not to purify the wicked dead in order that they might be brought to repentance and faith with the result that they will all be finally saved, as those teach who advocate the universal restoration of the entire human race. They are for the punishment of Satan and his fallen angels, and for those of the human race who enter eternity in a lost condition. Matthew 25:46 has been dealt with above.

As to Mark 3:29, the best Greek texts have "sin" instead of "damnation," which latter word appears in the A.V., as the translation of a Greek word meaning "judgment," and which is a rejected reading. The words "in danger of" are from a Greek word which refers to anyone "held in anything so that he cannot escape." Thus the one who committed the sin referred to in this passage is in the grasp of an eternal sin, the sin being eternal, not in the sense of eternally repeating itself, but in that it is eternal in its guilt. Such a sin demands eternal punishment. In II Thessalonians

1:9 we have "everlasting destruction." The Greek word translated "destruction" does not mean "annihilation." Moulton and Milligan define its first century Biblical usage as follows: "ruin, the loss of all that gives worth to existence." Thayer in his lexicon gives the meanings "ruin, destruction, death." The word comes from the verb meaning "to destroy." But to destroy something does not mean to put it out of existence, but to ruin it, to reduce it to such form that it loses all that gave worth to its existence. One may burn down a beautiful mansion. The materials which composed it are still in existence, a heap of ashes, but it is destroyed in that it cannot be used as a home any more. It is in such form that it has lost all that gave worth to its existence as a mansion. The eternal condition of the lost will be one of utter ruin, a condition in which the soul lives forever in a state devoid of all that makes existence worthwhile.

In Hebrews 6:2 we have "eternal judgment." The word "judgment" here is from a Greek word that refers to a condemnatory sentence, *aionios* being used to teach that this sentence is eternal in that the punishment it prescribes is unending. In Jude 7 we have lost human beings condemned to the same everlasting fire which has been prepared for Satan and the fallen angels, the latter in verse 6 being reserved for the Great White Throne judgment and the fire prepared for them (Matt. 25:41).

We come now to the passages in which *aion* is used. Because *aionios* describes the same future punishment which *aion* does, *aion* here cannot mean "a limited time," but "eternal," just as *aionios*. II Peter 2:17 tells us that "the mist of darkness" is reserved for those who reject the substitutionary atonement of the Lord Jesus. Jude 13 refers to those who like Cain refuse to place their faith in the blood of Jesus poured out on the Cross for sin, and who instead trust in their own good works. To these is reserved "the blackness of darkness forever." The expressions in Peter and Jude are from the same words in the Greek text, except that the best Greek manuscripts omit *aion* in the first passage. It however appears in the second which refers to the same darkness. The words "mist" and "blackness" come from one Greek word for "darkness," and the word "darkness" comes from another word meaning "darkness." Archbishop Trench in his *New Testament Synonyms* says this about the word translated "mist" and "blackness"; "The *zophos* (the former word) may be contemplated as a kind of emanation of *skotous* (the latter). It signifies in its first meaning the twilight gloom which broods over the regions of the setting sun, and constitutes so strong a contrast to the life and light of that Orient where the sun may be said to be daily new-born. . . . But it means more than this. There is a darkness darker still, that, namely, of the sunless underworld. . . . This too it further means, namely, that sunless world itself, though indeed this less often than the gloom which wraps it. . . . It will at once be perceived with what fitness the word in the New Testament is employed, being ever used to signify the darkness of that shadowy land where light is not, but only darkness visible." Such is the eternal fate of those who reject the precious blood of Jesus as the alone way of salvation from sin.

We come to Revelation 14:9-11 where the unsaved who worship the Wild Beast, namely, the Roman emperor who is Satan's regent in the revived Roman empire during the Great Tribulation, are said to be tormented, and where it is asserted that the smoke of their torment, that is, the smoke that issues from the cause of their torment, will ascend forever and forever, which means that their torment will be forever and forever. The Greek word translated "torment" was used in a secular document of the examina-

tion of slaves in the phrase "they under torture said."*
Thayer defines the word as follows, "to question by applying torture, to torture, to vex with grievous pains (of body
and mind), in the passive sense, to be harassed, distressed."
In Revelation 20:10, the eternal torment of Satan is spoken of. Thus, God's Word clearly teaches that the sufferings of the lost will be unending.

How this fact speaks to us of the infinite holiness, righteousness, and justice of God, and of the awfulness of sin.
But how it points us also to that Lonely Sufferer on Calvary's Cross, and brings to our ears the dreadful pathos of
that cry, "My God, my God, why hast thou forsaken me?"
What was it all for? The Lord Jesus suffered and died in
order that by satisfying the righteous demands of the law
which we violated, God might be able to offer us mercy
on the basis of justice satisfied. That mercy He offers you
now, unsaved reader, if you will accept it by faith in the
atoning work of His Son on the Cross. "For God so loved
the world, that He gave His Son, the only begotten one,
that whosoever believeth in Him might not perish but have
everlasting life." Put your trust in Him *now*, for tomorrow may be too late.

Moulton and Milligan.

VI.

Hell, Hades, and Tartarus

THERE are three Greek words in the New Testament translated by the one English word "hell," which fact results in some confusion in our thinking.

One of these is "Gehenna." It is the Greek representative of the Hebrew "Ge-Hinnom," or Valley of Hinnom, a deep narrow valley to the south of Jerusalem, where, after the introduction of the worship of the fire-gods by Ahaz, the idolatrous Jews sacrificed their children to the god Molech. After the time of Josiah, when this practice was stopped, it became the common refuse-place of the city, where the bodies of criminals, carcasses of animals, and all sorts of filth were cast. From its depth and narrowness, and its fire and ascending smoke, it became the symbol of the place of the future punishment of the wicked. The word is used in Matthew 5:22 in the phrase "the hell of fire," (Greek), and thus refers to the final abode of the wicked dead which is called in Revelation 19:20 "the lake of fire burning with brimstone." This lake of fire is in existence now, for the word "prepared" in the Greek of Matthew 25:41 is in the perfect tense which refers to a past completed action having present results. Hell had been already prepared and was in existence when Jesus spoke these words. There is no one there now. The first occupants of that dreadful place will be the Beast and the false prophet, Satan following them 1000 years afterwards. Then at the

Great White Throne Judgment, which occurs at the close of the Millennium, all lost human beings, the fallen angels, and the demons will also be sent there for eternity. Our word "hell" is the correct rendering of the word "Gehenna," and should be so translated in the following passages, Matthew 5:22, 29, 30; 10:28; 18:9; 23:15, 33; Mark 9:43, 45, 47; Luke 12:5; James 3:6.

The second of these words is "Hades," which is a transliteration, not a translation, of the Greek word. When we transliterate a word we take the spelling of that word over into another language in the respective letter equivalents, whereas when we translate a word, we take the meaning over into that language. The word itself means "The Unseen." This was the technical Greek religious term used to designate the world of those who departed this life. The Septuagint, namely, the Greek translation of the Old Testament, uses this word to translate the Hebrew "Sheol," which has a similar general meaning. The "Hades" of the pagan Greeks was the invisible land, the realm of shadow, where all Greeks went, the virtuous, to that part called Elysium, the wicked, to the other part called Tartarus.

The difference between the pagan and Biblical conceptions of Hades is that the former conceives of Hades as the final abode of the dead, whereas the latter teaches that it is the temporary place of confinement until the Great White Throne Judgment in the case of the wicked dead, and until the resurrection of Christ, in the case of the righteous dead, the latter since that event going at once to heaven at death (Phil. 1:23).

As the pagan conception of Hades included two parts, so the Biblical idea divided it into two parts, the one called paradise (Luke 23:43, but not II Cor. 12:4, and Rev. 2:7), or Abraham's bosom (Luke 16:22), for the righteous dead, and the other part for the wicked dead having no specific

designation except the general word "Hades" (Luke 16:23).
This Greek word is found in the following passages, to be
translated and interpreted generally as "Hades," the place
of the departed dead, and for the reason that the translators of the Septuagint use this word to express in the Greek
language what is meant in the Hebrew by the word "Sheol,"
the place of the departed dead.

In Matthew 11:23 and Luke 10:15, Capernaum is to be
brought down to the realms of the dead, presumably here
to that portion of Hades reserved for the wicked, because
of its rejection of the attesting miracles of our Lord. In
Luke 16:23, the rich man was in Hades, that part where the
wicked dead are kept until the judgment of the Great White
Throne. In Acts 2:27, 31, our Lord at His death went to
Hades, the passage in Acts being quoted from Psalm 16:,
where the Hebrew is "Sheol." His soul was not left in
Hades, the "paradise" portion, nor did His body in Joseph's
tomb see corruption, for He was raised from the dead on
the third day. He as the Man Christ Jesus, possessing a human soul and spirit, as He possessed a human body, entered
the abode of the righteous dead, having committed the keeping of His spirit to God the Father (Luke 23:46). The word
"grave" in I Corinthians 15:55 is not from the word
"Hades," for the best manuscripts have the word "death,"
while "Hades" is a rejected reading. The translation should
read, "death."

In Revelation 6:8, Death and Hades follow in the wake
of war and famine, Hades ready to receive the dead of the
Great Tribulation period. In Revelation 20:13, 14, Death
itself, and Hades with all the wicked dead are cast into the
lake of fire.

There are just two places where this Greek word should
be translated rather than transliterated. In Revelation
1:18, our Lord has the keys or control of The Unseen and

of death. That is, He is master of the unseen world which in the Christian system includes Hades, Tartarus, and the kingdom of Satan in the atmosphere of this earth.

The other place is Matthew 16:18 where we translate "The Unseen." The word "prevail" in the Greek means "to be strong to another's detriment, to overpower." The word "gates" is an orientalism for the idea of centralized legal authority. Lot sat in the gate of Sodom. Boaz went to the gate of Bethlehem to settle a legal matter with reference to his proposed marriage to Ruth. The word refers to a council. The word "hades" is out of the question here as an adequate translation, because the wicked dead in that place have no power to overcome the Church, and the righteous dead there at the time our Lord spoke these words had neither the desire nor power. The holy angels in heaven would have no such desire. All that is left in the unseen world are Satan and his demons. These constitute the Council in the Unseen that desires to bring about the destruction of the Church.

The third word translated "hell" is in II Peter 2:4 where the Greek word is "Tartarus," the prison of the fallen angels that sinned at the time of the flood (Gen. 6:1-4; I Peter 3:19, 20; Jude 6).

This brief study contains all the passages where the word "hell" is used in the New Testament, and can be used as a guide to the correct translation in each case.

VII.

The Christian's "Thanatopsis"

ONE OF the passages in the English translation which presents difficulties in interpretation is John 8:51, where our Lord says, "Verily, verily, I say unto you, If a man keep my saying, he shall never see death." We have called this "Golden Nugget," "The Christian's 'Thanatopsis'." The word "thanatopsis" comes from two Greek words which together mean "seeing death." Our Lord here presents the Christian view of death.

The assertion in the Greek is very strong. The idea is, "shall absolutely not see death." Then the statement is made stronger by the addition of a phrase which in other places in the New Testament is translated "forever." Thus, "If any man keep my saying, he shall absolutely not see death, never."

The key to the interpretation of the verse is found in the meaning of the word "see." There are six words in the Greek language which mean "to see." The first refers simply to the act of physical sight (Matt. 12:22). The second refers to physical sight that is accompanied by mental discernment (I John 1:1, "have seen"). The third means "to look upon, contemplate, view attentively," used, for instance, of a civilian watching a military parade (I John 1:1, "looked upon"). The fourth means "to scrutinize with the purpose of bringing about the betterment of the person so observed" (Hebrews 2:6, "visitest," Acts 20:28, "overseers"). The fifth word means "to fix one's eyes upon," metaph., "to fix one's mind upon one as an example" (Acts 3:4, "fastening his eyes upon him with John,"). Even Peter and John judged their beggars as to their worthiness to receive alms. The sixth word is the one used in John 8:51. It is used, primarily, not of an indifferent spectator, but of one who looks at a thing with interest and for a purpose. It expresses a fixed contemplation and a full acquaintance.

Now, the death spoken of here is physical death, for the Jews speak of Abraham as being dead, and our Lord does not correct them by saying that He was speaking of spiritual death. He therefore says that when a Christian is being put to sleep in Jesus (I Thess. 4:14, Greek), as he is dying, he will not look at Death with interest and for a purpose. He will be an indifferent spectator of Death, for he will have his eyes fixed on Jesus. The terrors of that awful thing called death, are not experienced by the one who puts his faith in the Lord Jesus. His attention will not be focused on death, nor will he feel its bitterness. This is what Paul means when he says (I Cor. 15:55), "O death, where is thy sting?" But those that go out of this life rejecting Him, have before them all the terrors of death. Oh, reader, are you sure that you are trusting in the precious blood of Jesus poured out in the substitutionary atonement on the Cross for you personally? We read in Hebrews 2:9 that Jesus tasted death for every man. That is, He not only died, but He experienced all the terror and bitterness of death in order that those who place their trust in Him as Saviour, will not experience the terror and bitterness of it all.

VIII.

A Pauline Paradox and Its Solution

THE Greek inscriptions show that many technical terms in pagan religions and in governmental circles of the first century A.D., are also found in the terminology of Christianity. For instance, the expression, "slave of the emperor," was in current use. There were imperial slaves all over the Roman world. This throws light upon Paul's claim to be a "bondslave of Jesus Christ" (Rom. 1:1), the word "servant" coming from a Greek word literally meaning "bondslave," the same Greek word being used in the inscriptions. Paul knew of this custom. The lord emperor was not only revered as a human ruler but also worshipped as a god. When Paul wrote these words to the Christians in the imperial city, he must have been conscious of the imperialistic challenge of Christianity proclaiming a Saviour whose bondslave he was, and who some day would come to displace the imperialism of Rome. Paul was some day to stand before Nero, not as a bondslave of the lord emperor, but as a bondslave of the King of kings, the One who came from the royal line of David.

Another such technical expression is found in I Corinthians 7:22, "the Lord's freeman." The title, "freedman of the emperor," is found frequently in the Greek inscriptions of the first century.

To be a bondslave of the emperor, was a position of servitude with a certain degree of honor attached to it, but to be the emperor's freeman, meant that the bondslave was liberated from that servitude and promoted to a position of a free man, which was a higher station. Paul in I Corinthians 7:22 says that the Christian is both the bondslave and the freeman of the Lord. How can he be both at the same time? The beautiful story can be told in three Greek words translated "bought" and "redeemed."

The first word means "to buy in the market place." It was used of the purchase of slaves. Sinners are bondslaves of Satan and sin (Rom. 6:17, 18; Eph. 2:2) We were purchased in the slave market, the price paid, the precious blood of Jesus. I Corinthians 6:20 uses this word. We were bondslaves of Satan, and we became bondslaves of Jesus Christ. A slave cannot say that he belongs to himself, but to his master. We belong to Christ. The word is also used in II Peter 2:1, where false teachers who deny the Lord who purchased them in the slave market, refuse to avail themselves of the high privilege of becoming His bondslaves. In Revelation 5:9, the saints in heaven are singing a song which speaks of the Lamb who bought them in the slave market to become His own bondslaves. Thus, Paul tells his readers that those who have put their trust in Jesus as Saviour, were purchased in the slave market, and are bondslaves of the coming King of kings (I Cor. 7:22, 23).

We are told in the same passage (I Cor. 7:22) that we are also the Lord's freemen. This brings us to the other words translated "redeemed." One means "to buy out of the market place." Galatians 3:13, which uses this word, tells us that we were purchased in the slave-market, but in such a way that while we are bondslaves of the purchaser, the Lord Jesus, we are never again to be put up for sale in any slave market. We have been bought out of the slave market. This means that we are bondslaves of the Lord Jesus forever. He will never sell us or permit us to be sold as slaves to anyone else. A bondslave of Jesus Christ never becomes a bondslave of Satan again.

The other word translated "redeemed" means "to release or liberate by payment of a ransom," and is used in I Peter 1:18; Titus 2:14. The noun having the same root means "ransom money used to liberate a slave." After our blessed Lord buys us in the slave market, the ransom money being His own precious blood, we become His private property. We are His bondslaves. Then He so arranges the details of the purchase that we will never be put up for sale in any slave market. He buys us out of the slave market. Then He sets us free. We are freemen, freed from the guilt, penalty, and power of sin, some day to be freed from the presence of sin. We are liberated from all that, so that we might realize in our lives that for which we were created, namely, to glorify God. It is the old story of the caged eagle, liberated to fly again in the pure air of the mountain tops. But how can we be His bondslaves and His freemen at the same time? After we have been purchased as His bondslaves, and have been liberated from our old master Satan, out of pure gratefulness of heart we say to our Lord, "Lord Jesus, we want to serve Thee as Thy bondslaves forever." Our position as His bondslaves is not one of compulsion, but of free will energized by an imparted divine nature and a supernaturally imparted love. Therefore, we are His bondslaves and His freemen at the same time, a thing impossible in the case of earthly slaves. Thus is solved one of the delightful paradoxes of Holy Scripture.

IX.

Paul the Scholar

SOMETIMES a very slight shade of meaning in a word
may speak volumes. Paul in Acts 22, is presenting his
defence before his fellow-countrymen. He states that he is a
man, Jewish by race, born in Tarsus of Cilicia, yet brought
up in Jerusalem at the feet of Gamaliel (22:3). Tarsus was
a city outside of Palestine, Greek in its culture. The fact
that Paul was born there would put him in an unfavorable
light with the Jerusalem Jews. We see that prejudice of the
Jews against their fellow-countrymen who had absorbed
Greek culture and who read the Old Testament in the Greek
Septuagint version rather than in their native Hebrew, man-
ifested in the early church (Acts 6), where those responsible
for the poor were neglecting the widows of men who were
pure-blooded Jews, yet who had imbibed Greek culture, and
therefore were called Grecians (6:1). But Paul was strictly
honest in recounting his life. He said, "born in Tarsus, . . .
yet brought up in this city." The word "yet" is from the
milder of two adversative particles in the Greek, both meaning "but." He could have used the stronger adversative.
Had he used the latter, he would have washed his hands of
Tarsus and all Hellenistic culture. But he could not hon-
estly do that. Saul of Tarsus had received training in the
Greek language and literature. Indeed, he was well read in
the latter, for in Acts 17:28 he quoted from two of the minor

Greek poets, Aratus and Cleanthes, and in Titus 1:12 from one of the Cretan poets. Anyone might have a smattering of Homer or Plato without being considered well trained, but to quote some minor writers, shows that Paul was a Jew of Hellenistic background. But that he also acquired a thorough training in the Hebrew Old Testament and in rabbinical lore, is seen clearly by another word he uses. He was educated at the feet of Gamaliel. He could have used either one of three prepositions each meaning "at." Had he used either of these, he would have had a position *before* the great teacher. But the preposition which he used means literally "beside, alongside," and carries with it the idea of close personal connection. Cannot you see the eager young man, Saul, seated close to his teacher, at his *side,* drinking in every word that fell from his lips? This may be a very small touch, but it speaks volumes. Paul was a scholar.

X.

Pauline Tactfulness

AN illustration of the tactfulness and delicacy of feeling of the apostle Paul is seen in his response to the gift which the Philippian saints sent to him, and which was the occasion for the letter. In 1:3-5 Paul says, "I thank my God . . . for your fellowship in the gospel from the first day until now." "Fellowship" is from a Greek word which means literally "to have in common with," and speaks here of the joint-participation of the Philippians with Paul in the gospel. The word "in" is from a preposition of motion, and thus speaks of progress. Thus Paul thanks God for the joint-participation of the Philippians in the progress of the gospel. The Philippian saints were joint-participants with Paul in the work of the gospel in that they helped supply his needs as he preached. They had been helping him from the first day when Lydia the purple dye seller had opened her home for the preaching of the gospel until that present moment when they had sent a gift to the great apostle who was in prison. In the Greek text the definite article "the" occurs before the adverb "now," which is a construction that we do not find in the English language. The definite article in Greek points out individual identity. It makes the thing referred to stand out in contrast to other things. Paul said that the Philippians had helped him in his missionary work from the first day until "the now." The word "now" refers to the time at which Paul wrote, but the article particularizes that time as being characterized by the receipt of the gift. "Now" is not a mere point in time, but a point in time whose character was marked by the receipt of the gift. The article is a delicate finger pointing to the gift without referring to it in so many words. Paul in the closing sentences of his letter (4:10-19) speaks of it in plain language, but he is so grateful for the gift that he cannot help but mention it at the very beginning. Yet with that rare tact and courtesy which was his, and which only our Lord can give, he thanked them for it without mentioning it by name. This joint participation of the Philippians in the progress of the gospel was the "good work" which God had begun in them. It was the grace of giving, and in this context, the grace of giving to missionary work.

XI.

Amalgamated Love

"SEEING ye have purified your souls in obeying the truth through the Spirit unto unfeigned love of the brethren, see that ye love one another with a pure heart fervently" (I Peter 1:22).

As one reads these words, the question arises as to why God exhorts saints who are already loving one another, to love one another. The answer to our question is found in the fact that the first word "love" comes from a Greek word referring to one kind of love, and the second word "love" is from another word speaking of a different kind of love.

The first word "love" is from a Greek word which speaks of that glow of the heart which is kindled by the perception of that in the object loved which affords one pleasure. Whatever in an object is adapted to give pleasure when perceived, tends to call out affection, and this affection is what this word expresses. The Greeks were very much occupied with the topic of friendship. This was an ideal word for the expression of this form of affection. The word is used in such expressions as, "to be in a friendly way at one's side," "to interest one's self in him in a friendly manner," "a man showed himself friendly to men by keeping open house." Thus this form of love is the response of the human spirit to what appeals to it as pleasurable. It speaks of a friendly affection.

This is the kind of love which these saints had for one another. This love was the result of their obedience to the truth through their dependence upon the Spirit. That is, their obedience to God's Word brought them all into right relationship to God in their personal lives, and into right relationship to one another in their fellowship with one another. This fellowship was a source of joy to them all, for the truth in the heart and life of each saint found its counterpart in and was attracted by the truth in the heart and life of the other saints. Each saint found in the heart of the other saint that which afforded him pleasure. He found a reflection of his own likes and dislikes, his own interests, his own thought-world in the life of his fellow-saint.

It is like the attraction which one artist has for another artist, or one musician, for another musician. This mutual attraction results in a mutual love awakened by the sense of pleasure one finds in the company of the other. So it was with these saints. They loved each other with a mutual reciprocal love because of the pleasure each had in the other's fellowship. It was a friendly love, a glow of the heart kindled by the perception of that in the other saint which afforded pleasure.

Now, this kind of love is a perfectly proper and legitimate love. But it is a love which is non-ethical. That is, it sets no standards of right and wrong. It does not include within its constituent elements, the idea of self-sacrifice in the interest of the one loved. It could therefore degenerate into something selfish and self-centered. One saint may find so much in another saint with which to gratify his desire for fellowship, that he does not think of the other person, but merely of himself and of his own welfare. Thus what started out as a mutual and friendly love, would become a selfish self-centered thing.

But God in His grace has provided a counter-balance which will make and keep this friendly love what it should be. The second use of the word "love" is from another Greek word. It speaks of that love which springs from an awakened sense of value in an object which causes one to prize the object loved. It expresses the love of approbation, of esteem, as over against the love of pure delight, which latter is our other word for love. It springs from an apprehension of the preciousness of the object loved. It derives its impulse more from the notion of prizing than of liking. It is a love which springs from the soul's sense of the value and preciousness of its object, and is the response of the heart to the recognized worth of the object loved.

Our first word is found frequently in the pagan Greek authors, but the second word is used very sparingly. This rather obscure word, used so infrequently in the pagan Greek writings, the New Testament writers as guided by the Holy Spirit select, and pour into it as into an empty receptacle, all the content of meaning we find in John 3:16 and I Corinthians 13, where it is used. It is the response of the heart of God to the preciousness of each lost human soul that results in the infinite love God shows at Calvary. Each human soul is precious, first, because it bears the image of its Maker, even though that image be marred by sin, and second, because, it is composed of material, if you please, which God can through redemption, conform to the very image of His beloved Son. Thus, this love is a love of self-sacrifice based upon the preciousness of the object loved.

God exhorts the saints who are already loving each other with a friendly love which is called out of their hearts because they find pleasure in each other's fellowship, to love each other also with a self-sacrificial love because of the preciousness of the saint who is loved, as precious to God as Christ is precious to Him. Thus, this friendly love is amalgamated with the love of self-sacrifice. The two are fused. The first is made a thing of heaven because it is purified, ennobled, elevated by the second.

Into this fellowship of the saints is introduced the love that sacrifices for the blessing of the other, the love that suffers long, the love that is kind, the love that does not envy, the love that does not vaunt itself and is not puffed up, the love that does not behave itself unseemly, the love that does not seek its own, the love that is not provoked, that thinks no evil, that does not rejoice in iniquity but rather in the truth, the love that bears, believes, hopes, and endures all things, the love that never fails.

This love is the love spoken of in Galatians 5:22, produced in the heart of the saint who is definitely subjected to the Holy Spirit, by the Holy Spirit Himself. This is the love that God is. This is the love that should saturate the friendly love which saints have for each other. Without it, the fellowship of the saints with one another becomes a selfish unsatisfactory thing, but amalgamated with it, this friendly love becomes a thing of heaven. The secret of the fullness of this divine love, is in the fullness of the Holy Spirit. And this is why God exhorts saints who are already loving one another, to be loving one another.

The translation reads as follows: "Wherefore, having purified your souls by means of your obedience to the truth, resulting in not an assumed but genuine love for the brethren, love that springs from your hearts by reason of the pleasure you take in them, from the heart love each other with an intense reciprocal love that springs from your hearts because of your estimation of the preciousness of your brethren, and which is self-sacrificial in its essence."

XII.

The Word "VISIT" in the New Testament

BY our English word "visit" we usually mean "the act of calling to see another, of paying a visit in the sense of a social call." Consequently we sometimes attach this meaning to the word when we find it in Scripture. But the Greek word of which it is the translation means something more than that.

The word "visit" is the translation of two closely related verbs which have the following meanings: first, "to look upon or after, to inspect, to examine with the eyes;" second, "to look upon in order to help or benefit, to look after, to have a care for, to provide for." The word "visit" is possibly the best single word translation of the Greek words, but the English reader can see that it does not adequately translate it. Take for instance, "Sick and in prison and ye visited me not" (Matt. 25:43). What a richer, fuller meaning we have when we go to the Greek text. It was no mere social call that would have met the need of the prisoner. Oriental prisons sometimes were cold and uncomfortable. Paul writes to Timothy from his prison in Rome, "The cloke that I left at Troas with Carpus, when thou comest, bring with thee" (II Tim. 4:13). What a prisoner needed was ministering care like the help which the Philippians sent to Paul by Epaphroditus. Truly, the latter's visit to Paul in his Roman prison is a good illustration of the meaning of the Greek word translated "visit" in Matthew 25:43.

Zacharias, at the birth of his son John the Baptist, knowing that the latter would be the forerunner of the Messiah
who would therefore shortly come, said, "Blessed be the
Lord God of Israel; for He hath visited and redeemed His
people" (Luke 1:68). When he used the word "visited," he
really said "for He has looked upon His people in order to
help and benefit them, and provide for them." Then in
Luke 1:78 he said, "The day-spring from on high hath
visited us." That Dayspring is none other than the Lord
Jesus, who looked upon Israel and had a care for His chosen
people so that He came to their aid. And when Israel refused the aid of its Messiah, He laments over Jerusalem and
its inhabitants, and speaks of its destruction, closing with
the words "Thou knewest not the day of thy visitation"
(Luke 19:44). The word "visitation" is from a noun whose
root is the same as the stem of our verb. Israel did not per-
ceive that the coming of Jesus of Nazareth was the day
when God was looking upon His people in order to help
them. We have the same meaning in Luke 7:16.

The verb form is used of Moses in Acts 7:23 where Stephen
speaks of him leaving the palace of Pharaoh to visit his
Jewish brethren who were the slaves of the Egyptian king.
"It came into his heart" to look after his brethren in order
to help them. He had the consciousness that he was the
God-ordained instrument to deliver Israel, and he was going
to its aid.

In Acts 15:14 we have a very significant statement, "Sim-
eon hath declared how God for the first time (in the house
of Cornelius) did visit the Gentiles, to take out of them a
people for His name." And so we could translate more fully
"how God for the first time did look upon the Gentiles in
order to help them and provide for them." After the first
missionary journey, Paul said, "Let us go again and visit our
brethren in every city where we have preached the word of

the Lord, and see how they do" (Acts 15:36). Paul's use of the verb "visit" included a tour of inspection and the giving of spiritual aid where that was needed.

In Hebrews 2:6 we have, "What is man, that thou art mindful of him? or the son of man, that thou visitest him?" The words "son of man" are here a designation of the human race. The Psalmist exclaims at the wonder of it all, that considering the insignificance of man, God would look upon him in order to help him and give him aid. I Peter 2:12 speaks of the fact that the unsaved who have been attracted to the Lord Jesus by the beautiful lives of Christians, and have put their faith in Him, will "glorify God in the day of visitation." The word translated "visitation" is allied to our verb, and refers to the day when God looks after them and cares for their souls in salvation. In I Peter 2:25, the word "Bishop" is from another word closely allied to the same verb. Thus God becomes the Bishop of the souls of the saints in that He looks after their spiritual welfare and gives them aid. In James 1:27 we have, "Pure religion and undefiled before God and the Father is this, To visit the fatherless and widows in their affliction, and to keep himself unspotted from the world." Here again, the word "visit" does not refer to a social call, but to the act of looking after the fatherless and the widows in order to help them.

The noun forms of this word are found in the following places and are translated by the words "overseer or bishop;" Acts 20:28; Philippians 1:1; I Timothy 3:1, 2; Titus 1:7; I Peter 2:25; and Acts 1:20 where the word "bishopric" should be translated "overseership." The word has the following meanings, "an overseer, one charged with the duty of seeing that things to be done by others are done rightly, a guardian." In the case of a church officer called a "bishop," it means "one charged with the spiritual oversight and welfare of the local church, with the responsibility of giving spiritual help to the saints."

As a result of this study, the English reader can understand more clearly the passages where the word "visit" is found.

XIII.

Here and There in the New Testament

PAID IN FULL. Our Lord in Matthew 6:2 is speaking of hypocrites of His day who blew a trumpet in the synagogues and streets to call men's attention to the alms they were giving, doing this in order that they may be glorified by men. His comment on this procedure is "They have their reward." "Synagogue" is from a Greek word made up of a verb which means "to go," and a preposition which means "with" and signifies "fellowship." Thus the composite word refers to the action of people "going with one another," thus congregating in one place. The word became the name for the place of worship where the Jews congregated. The word "hypocrite" was used of an actor on the Greek stage, one who played the part of another. These who made a display of giving alms were hypocrites in the sense that they played the part of a generous person who out of a heart of love would give to the poor. But their motive in giving was to have men glorify them, not from a desire to help the needy. They were actors on the stage of this life. They received the applause of the audience. Jesus said, "They have their reward."

The word "have" is from the verb which means "to have," and a prefixed preposition which means "off" and implies separation. The combined idea is "to have off." It speaks of the possession of something which is a full and final payment. It came to mean "I have received in full." It was the

technical expression regularly used in drawing up a receipt.
Paul used it when he said (Phil. 4:18) "I have all." He
was acknowledging the gift of the Philippians brought by
Epaphroditus, and sending them a receipt for the same. The
Greek secular non-literary manuscripts give instances of its
use all over the Hellenistic world. Our Lord's words could
be translated "They have received their reward in full."
These hypocrites had been paid in full, and they had no
further claim for reward. So is it when we do Christian work
to be seen of men, when we exalt ourselves instead of the
Lord Jesus. We are paid in full on earth, our pay, the
plaudits of men. We have no reward awaiting us over
yonder.

PLAYING TRUANT. In II Thessalonians 3:11, Paul
speaks of certain Christian men in the local church who
were walking disorderly. The English word "disorderly"
means "confused, unmethodical, turbulent, unruly." But
none of these meanings exactly fits the Greek word of which
it is the translation. The use of the Greek word is clearly
seen in an early account of a father who apprenticed his son
to a weaver for one year. The contract provided for the
details of food and clothing for the period of apprenticeship. Then the contract stated that if there were any days
on which the boy *failed to attend* or *played truant,* the
father must see that the boy report for work an equivalent
number of days after the apprenticeship was over. The
word translated "disorderly" is the Greek word in the contract which means "to play truant." These Thessalonian
saints were playing truant from their daily employment.
The occasion for this is suggested in the context where Paul
says, "The Lord direct your hearts into the love of God,
and the patient waiting for Christ." The doctrine of the
immanent return of the Lord Jesus for His Church was
firmly believed in this church. The saints looked from day

to day for that event. Some argued, of course wrongly, that
if the Lord might come the next day, that there was no
need for earning one's daily bread. But Paul, who had
taught them this great truth of the immanency of the Lord's
return, and whose expectation was just as intense as that
of the Thessalonian saints, calls their attention to the fact
that he worked for his daily bread in order that he might
not be obligated to anyone for support. His rule was that
if anyone did not work, he should not eat. He defines what
he means by "disorderly" in the words "working not at all."
Thus, the context agrees with the first century usage of the
word, "to play truant."

CALLED CHRISTIANS. It was at Antioch that the
disciples were first called Christians (Acts 11:26). The
name was coined by the pagans of the first century to iden-
tify the followers of the Christ from those who worshipped
the Roman emperor who was called Caesar. The word
"disciple" is the translation of a Greek word meaning
"one who learns." The word does not include within its
meaning the idea of salvation. Thus, the disciples of the
Christ could be either saved or unsaved. They merely had
to be followers of Him, those who were under His instruc-
tion and adhered to Him as a leader or teacher. Judas was
the one disciple of the twelve who was not a true believer.
In John 6:66 we have, "From that time many of his disciples went back and walked no more with him." They
followed our Lord in His ethical teachings, but when He
spoke of salvation through faith in a substitutionary blood
sacrifice, they parted company with Him. Therefore, one
must consult the context in which the word "disciple" is
found, to find out whether the disciple mentioned is saved
or unsaved.

Here we have the case of many people following the Lord
who were known as His disciples. The pagan world called

them "Christians." The Roman State was built around the Emperor not merely as the political but the religious head of the empire. Not only did the subjects of the empire render allegiance to the Caesar as the governing head, but they worshipped him as a god. Emperor worship, or as it is sometimes known, the Cult of the Caesar, bound together the empire's far-flung colonies and widely different peoples. These followers of the Caesar, members of the Cult of the Caesar, were called in the Greek language, *Kaisarianos*, followers of the *Kaisar* or Caesar.

Now appears a rival claimant to world worship and dominion, the Christ of Israel. There was a widespread consciousness in the Gentile portion of the race that some day there would appear in Israel, a great leader, called the Messiah. This was probably part of the knowledge which the Magi had when they came to worship the new-born King of the Jews (Matt. 2:1-11). While He was not well known during His life-time on earth, a fact which is attested by the meagre notice given Him by the historians of His day, yet when the Gospel of Grace was being preached throughout the Roman empire, and He was being proclaimed as the Christ, with all that that name involved, Rome took notice. The name "Christ" is the English spelling of the Greek word *Christos*, which in turn is the translation of the Hebrew word "Messiah." It was the Messiah who had died, and had risen again, who was described as the sinner's Saviour, and a king in His own right, coming from the famous line of Jewish kings, the Davidic. Here was a rival King and Priest, claiming the allegiance of the subjects of Rome. Those who put their faith in Him necessarily had to sever their allegiance to the ruling Caesar, so far as worshipping him was concerned. These who were once *Kaisarianos*, followers of the Caesar, now were known as *Christianos*, followers of the Christ.

Thus, the Roman world was divided into two rival cults, the Cult of the Caesar, and the Cult of the Christ.

Paul, speaking of the Christ (the definite article appears before "Christ" in the Greek, indicating that the term "Christ" was well-known) before Agrippa the Roman ruler, preached the gospel to him (Acts 26). Agrippa says to Paul, "Almost thou persuadest me to be a Christian." The literal Greek here is, "With but little persuasion thou wouldest fain make me a Christian." Agrippa scoffed at the idea of becoming a Christian. He was a proud *Kaisarianos,* a worshipper of the Caesar. He knew that he would lose his government position and his head also if he ever renounced his allegiance to Caesar in order to become a *Christianos.*

The name "Christian" was a term of reproach in the Roman world. It was the name of the members of that despised and hated sect which worshipped the Christ. Peter in his first epistle (4:16) says, "If any man suffer as a Christian (a *Christianos*), let him not be ashamed; but let him glorify God on this behalf." Thus, the persecution of the early Christians by Rome arose out of the antagonism of the empire against a rival supremacy, that of the Cult of the Christ.

The world coined the term, but the Holy Spirit in I Peter takes it up as one of the designations of a believer in the Lord Jesus. In the first century it designated those who worshipped the Christ and refused to worship the image of the emperor. How that reminds us of John's exhortation in his first epistle (5:21), "Little children, keep yourself from idols." That injunction applies to Christians today. An idol today is anything that a Christian might possess that is not in harmony with what the Lord Jesus is, anything that occupies a place in his life which has a tendency to exclude Christ. We have no Roman emperor today whom the State might direct us to worship. But let us keep a watchful eye open for the little idols that would keep us from the closest fellowship with and usefulness to our Lord.

In the Great Tribulation period, the Roman empire is again to rear its head. Emperor worship will be restored, and thus the Cult of the Caesar (Rev. 13). The Jewish remnant of 144,000 (Rev. 7:1-8) will proclaim the coming of the Christ, and the two rival supremacies will again be present in a revived Roman empire. There will be the *Kaisarianos* and the *Christianos,* the followers of Caesar and the followers of the Christ. But the personal advent of the Christ will displace the supremacy of the Caesars, and His Messianic rule will bring universal righteousness, peace, and prosperity to this earth.

REBUKE and REPROVE. These two words are the usual translations of two closely related words in the Greek text. When we keep in mind the distinction between these Greek words, a flood of light is thrown upon the passages in which they occur.

The word "rebuke" is the general translation of the word *epitimao*. This word is used when one rebukes another without bringing the one rebuked to a conviction of any fault on his part. It might be because the one rebuked was innocent of the charge, or that he was guilty, but refused to acknowledge his guilt. Examples of the first are seen in the action of Peter rebuking the Lord Jesus (Matt. 16:23), the disciples rebuking the children for accepting the blessing of our Lord (Matt. 19:13), and the crowd rebuking the blind man for calling upon Jesus (Luke 18:39). Illustrations of the second are found in the case of the repentant robber rebuking his fellow malefactor (Luke 23:40), and Jesus rebuking the demon (Mark 9:25), neither rebuke having any effect upon the recipient.

The second word is *elegcho* and is usually translated by the word "reprove." This word speaks of a rebuke which results in the person's confession of his guilt, or if not his confession, his conviction of his sin. The word is used in Job 5:17 (Septuagint). "Behold, happy is the man whom God *correcteth*." It is God's reproof of His own that results in conviction of sin and their confession. "Reprove" in Proverbs 19:25 (Septuagint) is from *elegcho*. The person who has spiritual understanding will respond to a rebuke from God by acknowledging his guilt and confessing it.

Our Lord uses the word when He says, "Which of you *convinceth* me of sin?" (John 8:46). *Elegcho* is the correct word here, for it was used in the Greek law courts not merely of a reply to an opposing attorney, but of a refutation of his argument. No one could prove any charges of sin against our Lord. No one could bring charges against Him in such a way as to convince Him that He was guilty.

But what a flood of light is shed upon the great passage, "And when he (the Holy Spirit) is come, he will reprove the world of sin, and of righteousness, and of judgment" (John 16:8). What a commentary upon the work of the Holy Spirit in the case of the unsaved whom He brings to a saving faith in the Lord Jesus. Here *epitimao* would not do, for the unsaved are not guiltless nor do those whom the Holy Spirit reproves, refuse to acknowledge and confess their guilt. The word "world" here must be interpreted in a limited way because of *elegcho*. The word here refers to those of the unsaved who are brought by the Holy Spirit into the place of salvation. The reproof spoken of is an effectual one. The rest of the unsaved hate the light and do not come to the light, lest their deeds be proven to be evil and they be put under obligation to confess their guilt (John 3:20). With the help of these definitions and illustrations of *epitimao* and *elegcho*, the student of the English Bible is now prepared to study for himself the passages in which each is found.

Epitimao occurs in the following places and is translated in the A.V., by the words "rebuke" and "charge": Matthew 8:26, 12:16, 16:22, 17:18, 19:13, 20:31; Mark 1:25, 3:12, 4:39, 8:30, 32, 33, 9:25, 10:13, 48; Luke 4:35, 39, 41, 8:24, 9:21, 42, 55, 17:3, 18:15, 39, 19:39, 23:40; II Timothy 4:2; Jude 9.

Elegcho is found in the following places and is translated by the words "reprove, convict, tell a fault, convince": Matthew 18:15; Luke 3:19; John 3:20, 8:9, 46, 16:8; I Corinthians 14:24; Ephesians 5:11, 13; I Timothy 5:20; II Timothy 4:2; Titus 1:9, 13, 2:15; Hebrews 12:5; James 2:9; Revelation 3:19.

BASTAZO. This is one of the many colorful words in the Greek New Testament. It has a variety of meanings; *to take up with the hands, to bear what is burdensome, to bear away, to carry off, to pilfer.* Moulton and Milligan in their *Vocabulary of the Greek Testament* report the following uses of the word. The word appears in a secular manuscript of A.D. 117 in a formula about taxation, where it has the sense of "endure." It appears in the sentence "No one will endure your cheek." How this latter phrase has remained with us. The Ephesian church could not bear (bastazo) them that are evil (Rev. 2:2, 3). It could not endure them in the same sense that no one could endure the cheek, the insults, sarcasm, gainsaying, cutting words, rudeness, and abuse of the unknown person mentioned in that early manuscript.

A document of the third century speaks of the Emperor Trajan granting an audience to rival Greek and Jewish emissaries from Alexandria, "each bearing (*bastazo*) their own unique, private gods." How like in usage is this to the words in Acts 9:15, "He (Paul) is a chosen vessel unto me, to bear (*bastazo*) my name before the Gentiles, and kings, and the children of Israel." Closely allied to this usage of *bastazo* is that found in a papyrus manuscript which contains a spell in which the words occur, "I *carry* the corpse of Osiris . . . should so-and-so trouble me, I shall use it against him." Compare Galatians 6:17 where Paul says, "From henceforth let no man trouble me: for I bear (*bastazo*) in my body the marks of the Lord Jesus." The word "marks" is from the Greek *stigma,* which comes over into the English language in our word "stigma," and means, "a mark pricked in or branded upon the body." According to ancient oriental usage, slaves and soldiers bore the name or stamp of their master or commander branded or pricked into their bodies to indicate to what master or general they belonged, and there were even some devotees who stamped themselves in this way with the token of their gods.

Thus, Paul says that he bears branded on his body, the scars and marks left there by the perils, hardships, imprisonments, beatings and scourgings he endured for the Lord Jesus, and which proved him to be a faithful soldier of Jesus Christ. Thus he could exhort Timothy to endure hardness as a good soldier of Jesus Christ (II Tim. 2:3). In our Galatian passage, he says in effect that he has suffered enough from the Judaizers who dogged his footsteps for many long years, and that his body scarred as the result of suffering for his Lord, should be enough to cause them to let him alone in his declining years and give him a little time of peace and rest. So, as the bearing (bastazo) of a particular amulet associated with the god Osiris was used as a charm against an adversary, so the scarred body of the apostle should be enough to dissuade the Judaizers from their continued attacks upon him. And just as these Greek and Jewish emissaries bore their own unique private gods before Trajan in their dress, language, actions, and testimony, so Paul was to do the same before the Gentiles, kings, and children of Israel.

A common use of *bastazo* was "to pilfer," throwing a flood of light on John 12:6 where Judas is said to have "had the bag, and *bare* (pilfered *bastazo*) what was put therein." In Matthew 3:11, we have "whose shoes I am not worthy to bear." *Bastazo* was firmly established in its usage of "to take off someone's sandals," and it has this meaning here. Compare Mark 1:7. It was not a question of wearing Messiah's sandals, but of taking them off for Him, a slave's duty. What humility on the part of John.

The word also meant "to bear what is burdensome," and is used in that meaning in the following places: Matthew 8:17, 20:12; Mark 14:13; Luke 7:14, 14:27, 22:10; John 10:31, 16:12, 19:17, 20:15; Acts 3:2, 15:10, 21:35; Romans 15:1; Galatians 5:10, 6:2, 5, 17; Revelation 2:2, 3. There is another Greek word which is the simple unqualified word meaning "to bear." When *bastazo* is used, the writer wishes to add some detail to the simple idea of carrying something. One should always look for that additional idea. The reader should study these places listed for the additional light which the word *bastazo* sheds upon the meaning of the passage. It will paint many a vivid picture in his mind's eye.

DEITY and DIVINITY. There are two Greek words translated "Godhead" in the New Testament, occurring but once each, *theiotes* and *theotes*. The Greek words are not however identical in meaning.

Paul uses the first in Romans 1:20, where he speaks of the fact that mankind can see the *theiotes* of God as it looks at the created universe. Trench observes, "Paul is declaring how much of God may be known from the revelation of Himself which He has made in nature, from those vestiges of Himself which men may everywhere trace in the world around them. Yet it is not the personal God whom any man may learn to know by these aids: He can be known only by the revelation of Himself in His Son; but only His

divine attributes, His majesty and glory . . . It is not to be
doubted that St. Paul uses this vaguer, more abstract, and
less personal word, just because he would affirm that men
may know God's power and majesty . . . from His works,
but would *not* imply that they may know Himself from
these, or from anything short of the revelation of His eternal Word."

Peter in his second epistle (1:3) uses the word *theia*
which is closely allied to *theiotes,* to describe God's power.
The word is translated "divine" in the A.V. Paul uses
theion in Acts 17:29 where it is translated "Godhead." In
Romans 1:20 he is speaking of what may be known of God
through nature. In his message to the Greek philosophers
at Athens, he argues that the fact that we are the offspring
of God by creation, gives us a picture, though inadequate,
of what God is like. However, He cannot be known in a
personal way through this means. Thus, in these passages,
he is speaking of the divine aspects of Deity, but not of Deity
as in itself absolute. The word *theiotes* was used in classical
Greek to speak of something in which there was a manifes-
tation of the divine, of some divine attributes, but never of
absolute deity. The word was used when a human being
was raised to the rank of a god. He was therefore divine.
But absolute deity was never ascribed to him by this word.
The word *theiotes* should therefore be translated in such a
way as to bring out the thought of divinity, namely, that
state of being in which the individual has divine character-
istics. Paul in Romans 1:19 uses the Greek word *theos*
which speaks of absolute deity, and then in the next verse
says that the created universe shows His eternal power and
divinity, using *theiotes.*

The other word *theotes* occurs in Colossians 2:9, where
Paul says that "In him (the Lord Jesus) dwelleth all the
fulness of the Godhead bodily." The Greek is very strong

here. One could translate, "For in Him corporeally there is permanently at home all the fulness of the Godhead." That is, in our Lord Jesus in His incarnation and in the permanent possession of His human body now glorified, there resides by nature and permanently the fulness of the Godhead. The word "Godhead" is from our second word *theotes*. The word expresses Godhead in the absolute sense. *It is not merely divine attributes that are in mind now, but the possession of the essence of deity in an absolute sense.* The Greek Fathers never use *theiotes* but always *theotes* as alone adequately expressing the essential Godhead of the three several Persons in the Holy Trinity. The Latin Christian writers were not satisfied with *divinitas* which was in common use, but coined the word *deitas* as the only adequate representative of the Greek word *theotes*.

In these days when translators of the modernistic school will render the last sentence of John 1:1 "And the Word was divine," translating the word *theos* which means "absolute deity" by the word "divine," it behooves those who believe in the absolute deity of the Lord Jesus, to use the expression "deity of Jesus Christ," rather than "divinity of Jesus Christ." Paul never spoke of the divinity of Jesus Christ, always of His deity. Our Lord does have divine attributes, but He is also God the Son, possessing the same essence as God the Father, and is co-equal with the other two members of the Trinity in His deity.

BAPTIZE UNTO REPENTANCE. John the Baptist makes the statement, "I indeed baptize you with water unto repentance" (Matt. 3:11). Peter says, "Repent, and be baptized everyone of you in the name of Jesus Christ for the remission of sins" (Acts 2:38). The word "unto" signifies "result." For instance, "I am not ashamed of the gospel, for it is the power of God unto salvation" (Rom. 1:16). The word "for" in our second text has the same meaning.

Are we to understand that water baptism as administered by John the Baptist and Peter, resulted in the repentance of those who were the recipients of it, in the face of the fact that repentance is a work of the Holy Spirit in the heart of the unsaved, this repentance being "unto life," that is, resulting in life (Acts 11:18)?

The words "unto" and "for" in Matthew 3:11 and Acts 2:38 are from the Greek preposition *eis*. Dana and Mantey in their excellent treatment of Greek prepositions based upon the papyri findings, give as one of the uses of this word, "because of."* This usage is found in Matthew 12:41 where the men of Nineveh repented *at* or *because* of the preaching of Jonah, and in Romans 4:20, where Abraham did not stagger in unbelief, because of the promise of God. In the case of the men of Nineveh, Jonah's preaching was the cause of their repentance. In the case of Abraham, the reason why he did not stagger in unbelief, was because of the promise of God. The word "stagger" here is from a Greek word which means "to vacillate between two opinions." Thus it was the repentance of those who received John's message which was the cause of their baptism. The same was true of Peter's at Pentecost. John's words were, "I indeed baptize you with water because of repentance," and Peter's, "Repent, and be baptized everyone of you in the name of Jesus Christ because of the remission of sins." That this is the correct translation and interpretation of our texts is also seen from the testimony of Josephus to the effect that John the Baptist baptized people only after they had repented: "Who (John) was a good man, and commanded the Jews to exercise virtue, both as to righteousness towards one another and piety towards God, and so to come to baptism; for that the washing (with water) would be acceptable to him, if they made use of it, not in order to

---

Manual Grammar of the Greek New Testament.

the putting away of some sins, but for the purification of
the body; supposing still that the soul was thoroughly purified beforehand by righteousness." John's words, "Bring
forth therefore fruits meet for repentance" (Matt. 3:8),
clearly show that he demanded some evidence of salvation
before he would baptize a person.

Thus, we have the scriptural meaning of water baptism.
It is the testimony of the person to the fact of his salvation.
The only proper recipient of water baptism therefore is one
who has received the Lord Jesus as his personal Saviour, and
is trusting in His precious blood for salvation from sin.

The Greek text thus clears up a difficulty found in the
English translation. Baptism is not the prerequisite of repentance, much less its cause, but the testimony of the one
who has entered the door of salvation.

XIV.

An Exposition of the Greek Text of Romans VI

PAUL wrote chapter six of Romans in answer to two questions: "Shall we continue in sin, that grace may abound?" answering this question in verses 2-14; and "Shall we sin, because we are not under the law, but under grace?" replying to this question in verses 15-23. These questions were raised, not by the apostle himself, but by his hearers in the first century who did not understand grace, and thus arrived at false conclusions concerning it.

Paul answers the first question by showing that such a thing is impossible, since God's grace makes provision for an inward change in the believer the moment he receives the Lord Jesus as his Saviour, a change in which the power of indwelling sin is broken and the divine nature implanted. This results in the liberation of that person from the compelling power of the Adamic nature, and his acquisition of the desire and power to live a holy life. This, Paul argues, makes impossible a life of sin.

He replies to the second question by asserting that a Christian does not take advantage of divine grace, since he has ceased to be a bondslave of Satan and has become a bondslave of the Lord Jesus, having a nature whereby he hates sin and shuns the Devil, and loves to serve the Lord Jesus.

In answering these objections to his teaching of pure grace without any admixture of law as a means of controlling the saint and causing him to live a life pleasing to God, Paul deals with the mechanical impossibility of going on in sin. We are occupied in Romans VI, not with the question of *what kind* of a life the child of God should live, a subject which he presents in chapters 12-16, but with the question of *how* or *by what method* the believer is to live that life. The reason why so many children of God who are earnestly trying to live a Christian life which would glorify the Lord Jesus, fail in that endeavor, is because they do not understand the truth of this chapter. Their experience is like that of Paul, who before he came into the truth of Romans VI said, "I am carnal, sold under sin. For that which I do I do not understand: for what I would, that I do not; but what I hate, that do I" (7:15). Paul uses three words to designate the three spiritual classes of men, the natural man (I Cor. 2:14), namely, the unsaved person; the carnal man (I Cor. 3:1), the Christian who is not living the victorious life; and the spiritual man (I Cor. 2:15), the Christian who understands God's prescribed method for the saint which results in his living a holy life. Our exposition of the Greek text of this wonderful portion of God's Word should, under the blessing of God the Holy Spirit, solve the problem of some dear child of God who is not getting consistent victory over sin. It therefore should prove an intensely practical study.

The first question found its occasion in Paul's statement in 5:20, "where sin abounded, grace did much more abound." The words "much more abound" are from a word referring to a superabundance of something with an additional supply added to this superabundance. Paul's teaching here is that no matter how much sin there might be committed, there are always unlimited resources of grace in the great heart of God by which to extend mercy to the sinning individual. The reaction of the heart that does not understand grace is seen in the question asked, "What shall we say then? Shall we continue habitually to live in the sphere and grip of the sinful nature, in order that this grace may be increasingly lavished in superabundant outgoings?" The verb used, refers to habitual action. The word "sin" refers here not to acts of sin, but to the sinful nature, since Paul is dealing here with the mechanics of the Christian life, not the outward actions of the individual.

His first answer to this question is "God forbid." The literal Greek is, "May it not become." He dismisses the very thought as unthinkable. One could translate, "far be the thought."

His second answer is, "How shall we who are dead to sin, live any longer therein?" The word "how," leaves no room for the possibility of the continued habit of sin in the Christian life, for the Greek word means "how is it possible?" "We" is from a word that not only refers to the individuals concerned, but also to the quality or character of these individuals. The fuller translation is "such as we." "Are dead" is from a past tense verb, which tense also speaks of finality, and we translate "died once for all." "Sin" is in a construction in Greek which causes us to translate "with reference to sin." The verb "live" is from a word which speaks here of the life principle, not the actions of the person. The translation thus far reads, "What shall we say then? Shall we habitually abide under the control of sin in order that this grace previously mentioned may be increasingly lavished in superabundant outgoings? Far be the thought. Such as we who died once for all with reference to sin, how is it possible for us to exist in the grip of its motivating energy any longer?"

But let us look at the word "died." Death is not extinction of being, but a separation. In the case of physical death, it is the separation of the individual from his physical body. In the case of spiritual death, it is the separation of the person from the life of God. Here the word refers to the separation of the believer from the power of the sinful nature. Before salvation, he was compelled to obey its behests. Since salvation, its power over him is broken. We must be careful to note that Paul is not teaching what is called "the eradication of the sinful nature," namely, that that nature is taken away completely. The Bible teaches that this nature remains in the believer until he dies (Rom. 7:18, 21; I John 1:8), but the believer is not in it in the sense of being in its grip. Thus Paul answers the question as to whether a Christian should continue in habitual sin, by stating its impossibility, and on the ground that that nature which before salvation made him sin habitually, has had its power broken. It is a mechanical impossibility. We paraphrase the question: "Such as we who have been separated once for all from the power of the sinful nature, how is it possible for us to continue to exist in the grip of its motivating energy any longer?" Thus, when God justifies the believer, he also breaks the power of sin in the life. Grace does here what law never did. It not only forbids sin but also defeats its power in the person's life.

Then Paul proceeds to answer the question from another angle. In his first answer he showed the impossibility of habitual sin in a Christian's life by reason of the fact that the power of the sinful nature was broken when the believer was saved. Now he shows its impossibility in that the believer is made a partaker of the divine nature (II Peter 1:4). The life of God, surging through his being, causes him to hate sin and love holiness, and produces in him both the desire and the power to do God's will.

Paul speaks of this in Philippians 2:11, 12, where he says "Wherefore, my beloved, as ye have always obeyed, not as in my presence only, but now much more in my absence, carry to its ultimate goal your own salvation with fear and trembling, for God is the One who is constantly supplying you the impulse, giving you both the power to resolve and the strength to perform His good pleasure."

This truth Paul presents in verses 3 and 4 where we are taught that all believers were baptized into Jesus Christ and thus shared His death, in order that they also might share His resurrection life.

We look first at the phrase "baptized into Jesus Christ." It is set in a context of supernaturalism. In verse 2 we have the supernatural act of God breaking the power of indwelling sin for the believer. In verse 4 we have the supernatural act of God imparting divine life to the believer. Verse 3 reaches back to the action spoken of in verse 2 and forward to that spoken of in verse 4. We were baptized into Jesus Christ so that we might be baptized into His death on the Cross, in order that through our identification with Him in that death, we might die with reference to sin, that is, have the power of indwelling sin broken. We were also baptized into His death so that we might share His burial, and thus His resurrection, and in that way have His divine life imparted to us. Thus this baptism accomplished two things. It resulted in the power of sin being broken and the divine nature being implanted, which operation took place at the moment the believer placed his faith in the Lord Jesus. Therefore, since the results were operative in the believer the moment he was saved, the baptism into Jesus Christ in which that person shared His death, burial, and resurrection, must have taken place, potentially, previous to his being saved, and actually, at the moment of salvation. Our Lord died, was buried, and arose almost 2000 years ago. In the mind and reckoning of God, each believer was in Christ then, in order that he might when he believed, participate in the benefits which His death, burial, and resurrection brought forth. Therefore, the baptism referred to here is not water baptism, but the baptism by means of the Holy Spirit (I Cor. 12:13). Let it be said in passing, that the writer believes in the ordinance of water baptism as obligatory upon all believers on the Lord Jesus Christ, that it is their testimony to the fact of their salvation, and he finds plenty of scriptural warrant for it elsewhere. No ceremony of water baptism ever introduced a believing sinner into vital union with Jesus Christ. Furthermore, many true children of God never have fulfilled their obligation of testifying to their salvation in water baptism. And who is prepared to deny that they have been united to Christ? Paul is concerned here with the supernatural working of God resulting in an inner change in the spiritual mechanics of the believer's life, and as a clear thinker who stays within the compass of his subject, Paul does not introduce the symbol where the supernatural alone is in view.

But how are we to understand the word "baptism"? This word is the spelling in English letter equivalents of the word *baptisma,* the verb of the same stem being *baptizo.* The Greek word has two distinct uses, a mechanical one, and a ritualistic one, to be determined by the context in which it is found. Since the word "baptism" is only the spelling of the Greek word *baptisma,* and not a word native to the English language, it has no meaning of its own and therefore must derive its meaning from the Greek word of which it is the spelling. Furthermore, it must be interpreted and translated in its two meanings just as the Greek word is. We will present usages of the Greek word as found in classical Greek, and in the Koine Greek of secular documents, the Septuagint, and the New Testament.

For the following instances of the purely mechanical usage of *baptizo* in classical Greek, I am indebted to my honored and beloved teacher of Greek at Northwestern University, Professor John A. Scott, Ph.D., LL.D., classical Greek scholar who in the field of classical criticism has refuted the theory of Frederick August Wolf, who claimed that the Iliad and Odyssey were not written by the poet Homer but are a composite of the poetic expression of the Greek people, publishing the results of his findings in his book, *The Unity of Homer,* and who in the field of New Testament criticism has written the book, *We Would Know Jesus,* in which he demonstrates the historical accuracy of the four Gospels as confirmed by contemporary records, thereby rendering valuable assistance to the cause of evangelical Christianity in view of the destructive tendencies of that which passes for present day criticism of the New Testament: "The first use of *baptizo* is in the ninth book of the Odyssey, where the hissing of the burning eye of the Cyclops is compared to the sound of water where a smith dips, *baptizes,* a piece of iron, tempering it. In the Battle of the Frogs and Mice it is said that a mouse thrust a frog with a reed, and the frog leaped over the water, baptizing it with its blood. Euripides uses the word of a ship which goes down in the water and does not come back to the surface. Lucian dreams that he has seen a huge bird shot with a mighty arrow, and as it flies high in the air it baptizes the clouds with its blood. An ancient scholium to the Fifth Book of the Iliad makes a wounded soldier baptize the earth with his blood. It is the ordinary word for staining or dyeing, and words derived from it meaning "dyer" and "dyes" are common. The most common meaning is to plunge into a liquid, but it is so common in other meanings that in each case the meaning must be determined by the context." In Xenophon's *Anabasis* we have an instance where the word *baptizo* has both a mechanical and a ceremonial meaning. Before going to war, the Greek soldiers placed (*baptizo*) the points of their swords, and the barbarians the points of their spears in a bowl of blood.

In secular documents of the Koine period, Moulton and Milligan report the following usages: "a *submerged* boat, ceremonial *ablutions,* a person *overwhelmed* in calamities, a person *baptizo* upon the head."

We have in Leviticus 4:6 the words, "And the priest shall dip his finger in the blood, and sprinkle of the blood seven times before the Lord," where "dip" is from *baptizo* and "sprinkle" is from *rantizo* (Septuagint), the first referring to the action of introducing the finger into the blood, and the second, speaking of the ritualism of sprinkling that blood.

In the New Testament we find the word translated "washings" in Hebrews 9:10, speaking of the ablutions of Judaism; referring to ceremonial washing of cups, pots, brazen vessels, and of tables (Mark 7:4); and to the ceremony of water baptism (Matt. 3:7, 16; John 4:1; Acts 16:33; I Corinthians 1:14; I Peter 3:21). A purely mechanical usage is seen in Luke 16:24 where the rich man asks that Lazarus dip (baptize) his finger in water and cool his tongue.

The usage of the word as seen in the above examples, resolves itself into the following definition of the word *baptizo* in its mechanical meaning: "the introduction or placing of a person or thing into a new environment or into union with something else so as to alter its condition or its relationship to its previous environment or condition." And that is its usage in Romans VI. It refers to the act of God introducing a believing sinner into vital union with

Jesus Christ, in order that that believer might have the power of his sinful nature broken and the divine nature implanted through his identification with Christ in His death, burial, and resurrection, thus altering the condition and relationship of that sinner with regard to his previous state and environment, bringing him into a new environment, the kingdom of God. That is what Paul refers to when he says, "hath translated us into the kingdom of the Son of His love" (Col. 1:13). We have this same mechanical usage of *baptizo* in I Corinthians 12:13, "For by means of the instrumentality of one Spirit were we all baptized into one body," where Paul speaks of the act of the Holy Spirit placing or introducing the believing sinner into the body of Christ, as in our Roman text he refers to the same act, but speaks of the Head of the Body rather than the Body itself. The word "Spirit" is in the instrumental case, which case designates the means by which the action in the verb is accomplished. The Holy Spirit is the divine agent who Himself baptizes (introduces) the believer into vital union with the Lord Jesus. It should be clear from this that the baptism by means of the Spirit is not for power. Its sole purpose is to unite the believing sinner with his Saviour. Power for holy living and for service comes from the fullness of the Spirit. The baptism is an act which takes place at the moment the sinner believes, never to be repeated. The fullness is a moment by moment continuous state as the believer trusts the Lord Jesus for that fullness (John 7:37, 38).

We are now ready for the further examination of verses 3 and 4. The words "so many of us as" in the Greek, do not imply that some were not baptized, but designate all collectively. This is checked up by I Corinthians 12:13 in the statement "were we all baptized." This again points to the fact that Paul is speaking here of the baptism by the

Spirit, for all believers are in Christ, and yet all have not fulfilled their obligation of conforming to the ordinance of water baptism. The words "know ye not," in the original are literally "or are ye ignorant?", the Greek showing that the persons addressed were not ignorant of these facts, but conversant with them. The word "into" is from a Greek word which denotes an "inward union." The translation is as follows: "Or, are ye ignorant of the fact that all we who were baptized (introduced) into an inward union with Christ Jesus, into (a participation in) His death were baptized (introduced)?"

We now consider verse 4. The words "newness of life" do not refer to the new kind of life we are to live before the world. They do not refer to our Christian testimony as seen in our thoughts, words, and deeds. They speak of the new life implanted which is a motivating energy, providing both the desire and the power to live a Christian life. We are to walk, that is, conduct ourselves in the power of the new life which is imparted to us in regeneration. Whereas, before salvation, we walked in the power of the Adamic nature which gave us the desire and power to sin, we now are to walk in the energy of the new life God has imparted, which gives us both the desire and power to live a holy life. The translation is as follows: "Therefore, we were buried in company with Him through the intermediate instrumentality of this baptism (introduction) into His death, in order that even as Christ was raised out from among the dead through the glory of the Father, thus also we by means of a new life (imparted) should conduct ourselves," or, "thus also we from the power of a new life (imparted) should derive the motivating energy for our walk (thoughts, words, and deeds)."

To sum up verses 2-4: It is not possible for a saint to continue living a life of habitual sin, because the Holy

Spirit has baptized (introduced) him into vital union with Christ Jesus, this introduction having taken place potentially and in the mind and economy of God at the time our Lord died on the Cross, was buried in the tomb, and was raised from the dead, in order that the actual benefits of the believer's identification with Christ in these might be his at the moment he puts his faith in Jesus Christ as his Saviour, these benefits being the breaking of the power of indwelling sin and the impartation of the divine nature.

In verses 5-10 we have Paul's "in other words." He, master teacher that he is, seeks to make clearer his teaching in verses 2-4 by elaborating upon it in verses 5-10, and by presenting the same truth in a different way. We will look at verse 5. The word "if" in the Greek is not the conditional particle of an unfulfilled condition. It is a fulfilled condition here, its meaning being, "in view of the fact." "Planted" is from a compound word, one part of the word meaning, "to grow," and the other part implying close fellowship or participation on the part of two persons in a common action or state. The whole word speaks of an intimate and progressive union. The words "have been" are from a verb which speaks of entrance into a new state of existence. The verb is in the perfect tense, which tense in Greek speaks of an action completed in past time having present results. The word "likeness" speaks of a likeness which amounts well nigh to an identity. The translation so far is as follows: "For in view of the fact that we have become united with Him in the likeness of His death with the present result that we are identified with Him in His death." All believers from Adam's time to the time of the Great White Throne judgment were baptized (introduced into vital union) into the Lord Jesus when He died on the Cross. This vital union with Him resulted in our participating in His death, He dying a vicarious death in our behalf, we dying with reference to our sinful nature. In the case of our Lord, the result was that, having died once for all with reference to our sins, He will never die again (6:9). In the case of the believer, the result was that, having died once for all with reference to the sinful nature, he is forever delivered from its compelling power.

The words "we shall be," are "a future of logical result." They do not point to the future physical resurrection of the saint. Paul speaks of that in Romans 8:11. Here he is speaking of the spiritual resurrection of the believer which occurred potentially when Christ was raised out from among the dead, and actually, at the moment he believed. Thus, Paul argues that in view of the fact that believers have become united with Christ in the likeness of His death, the logical consequence of that identification with Christ in His death is identification with Him in His resurrection. The translation of verse 5 follows: "For, in view of the fact that we have become united with Him in the likeness of His death, with the present result that we are identified with Him in His death, certainly we also (as a necessary consequence) shall be in the likeness of His resurrection." As our Lord came out of the tomb in the same body in which He died, but with that body energized by a new life principle, (His precious blood having been poured out at Calvary, Levit. 17:11), and thus walked in newness of life, that is, walked in the energy of a new life, so the believer, identified with Him in His resurrection, leaves his old dead self in the tomb of his former life, and now walks in the energy of a new life principle surging through his being, the divine life imparted through his identification with Christ in His resurrection.

Paul now takes up this two-fold result in verses 6-10, the breaking of the power of the Adamic nature in verses 6-7, and the impartation of the divine nature in verses 8-10. We will look first at verses 6-7. The word "man" is not translated from the Greek word for "man" which refers to an individual male member of the human race, but from the word for "man" that is racial in its implications. It refers to the human race as contrasted to animals Here it refers to the individual man or woman, boy or girl, seen as a human being, a personality.

There are two words in Greek which mean "old." One refers to that which is old in the sense of having existed from the beginning, the emphasis being upon the length of time it has been in existence. The other refers to that which is antiquated, out of date, belonging to a world of has-been, worn out. The second is used here. The expression, "our old man," refers therefore to the old unrenewed self, that person which we were before salvation did its work in our being, a human being dominated entirely by the Adamic nature, having a heart darkened by sin, totally depraved in its entire being. It is the person when looked at from this side of salvation that is antiquated, out of date, belonging to a world of has-been.

The words "is crucified" are more properly, "was crucified," coming from a past-tense verb in the Greek. When we died with Christ, that old unregenerate totally depraved person we were before salvation died. The words "of sin" are in a construction in the Greek called "the genitive of possession." The body here is the physical body possessed by the sinful nature in the sense that the latter dominates or controls it. The word "destroyed" is from a Greek word which means "to render idle or inoperative, to put an end to, to make inefficient." The words "serve sin" are from the verb whose stem is the same as the noun translated "bond-slave." It refers to habitual slavery to something. Our translation reads: "Knowing this, that our old self was crucified with Him, in order that the body (then) dominated by sin might be rendered inoperative (in that respect), and this for the purpose that we should no longer be habitually rendering a slave's obedience to sin." Thus God has put an end to the domination of the sinful nature over the believer, and has rendered the physical body idle, inoperative, in that respect.

Verse 7 is an illustration of the truth taught in verse 6. The words "is dead," are from a past tense in the Greek which speaks of the fact of a past action, the tense also speaking of finality, and should be translated "died once for all." The word "freed" is from the Greek word which is usually translated "righteous" in its noun form, and "justify" in its verb. As a man who has died physically is freed from bondage to sin in which he was held, so a person who has died to sin in a spiritual sense, is released from its bondage. Thus the human body is released from bondage to sin in that the crucifixion of the old self results in the body being liberated from the power of sin. The word "freed" is in the perfect tense, which tense is so often used when the writer is speaking of God's work of salvation in the believer, since this tense speaks of a past completed action having present, and in a context where salvation is spoken of, fixed and permanent results. Verse 7 therefore reads "For he who died once for all is in a permanent state of freedom from sin."

Having dealt with the breaking of the power of the Adamic nature in verses 6-7, Paul now turns to the matter of the impartation of the divine nature in verses 8-10. The first is the negative aspect of sanctification, where provision is made for the defeat of the sinful nature. The second is the positive side of sanctification, where provision is made for the introduction of a new life, Christ Jesus Himself (Col. 3:4), into the being and experience of the believer.

We look first at verse 8. The "if" refers to a fulfilled condition. There is no doubt about the fact that each believer died with Christ. "Be dead" is again from a past tense verb speaking of an accomplished fact. "Believe" is not to be taken here in the sense of "trust," which sense it has in contexts where the believer's faith in the Lord Jesus is referred to, but in the sense of a dogmatic belief. It is a belief that rests upon the logic of "since such and such a thing is true, it naturally follows that such and such will be the case." The future "shall" is not "a future of time," but of "logical result." The words "live with Him" do not refer to any fellowship in the sense of companionship which the believer may have with the Lord Jesus either in this life or in eternity. The preposition "with" is followed by the pronoun "Him" in the instrumental case. This case in Greek speaks of the means whereby the action or the state represented in the verb is accomplished. The word "live" here speaks of, not the experience of the believer, but the motivating energy which determines his conduct. That motivating energy is a Person, the Lord Jesus. He is the Life by means of which we live our new lives. He is our new existence. This is exactly what Paul means when he says, "For to me to live is Christ" (Phil. 1:21).

The Christian life is not primarily a system of ethics to be obeyed, for which obedience there is supplied both the desire and power. It is a Person living His life in and through another person, "Christ in you, the hope of glory" (Col. 1:27). That is what Paul means when he prays that Christ might be formed in the saints (Gal. 4:19). The Greek word "form" has no idea of physical shape, or of moulding some solid substance, or of creating or producing something. It refers to the action of an individual giving outward expression of his true inward nature. Paul prays that the lives of the saints may be so yielded to the Lord

Jesus, that He may be able to give outward expression of His own glorious Person in the thoughts, words, and deeds of the believer in whose heart He lives. Thus, the believer is not only alive in salvation by virtue of the fact that Christ is his life, but he lives his Christian life in dependence upon Him, or by means of Him. That is what Paul means by the words, "shall live with Him." The translation reads, "Now, since we died once for all with Christ, we believe that we shall also live by means of Him." Thus, as we died in company with Christ on the Cross, so also we shall live in company with Him, participating in the same life which He possesses. We offer the following paraphrase, "Now, since we died once for all with Christ, we believe that as a necessary consequence, we shall also derive our spiritual existence and the motivating impulse for our Christian experience from Him."

Verses 9 and 10 are presented as the basis for the above assertion, namely, that since we died with Christ we shall also live with Him; "Knowing that Christ having been raised out from among the dead, dies no more; death no longer has dominion over Him, for the death which He died, He died with reference to sin once for all: but the life He now lives, He lives with reference to God." Thus, the believer died with reference to his sinful nature once for all, resulting in his deliverance from its power. He now lives with respect to the life of God. His new life is Christ.

In verses 1-10, Paul has replied to the question "What shall we say then? Shall we continue habitually to live in the sphere and grip of the sinful nature, in order that this grace may be increasingly lavished in super-abundant outgoings?," by asserting that the mechanical set-up in the inner being of the believer is different from that in the unbeliever. In the latter, the sinful nature has supreme and

absolute control. Nor does the unbeliever possess any goodness by nature which would combat the evil tendencies of
the evil nature and produce goodness in his life. All one
can expect from this mechanical set-up is a life of habitual
sin. But, Paul asserts, in the case of the believer, this mechanical set-up has been changed. The new set-up which
God installed is one in which the power of that sinful nature is broken, and one which includes the impartation of
the divine nature, which latter combats the evil tendencies
of the sinful nature (Gal. 5:17), and produces in the believer's life, the Christian graces (Gal. 5:22, 23). This
makes impossible a life of habitual sin.

This new spiritual machinery operates in every child of
God. But the degree of efficiency with which it works is de-
pendent upon the care which the believer bestows upon it.
An automobile engine under normal conditions will oper-
ate for a long time without any special attention. But if one
expects the highest degree of efficiency from it, he finds it
necessary to have a mechanic check over the various parts
at frequent intervals and make the adjustments and repairs
that are necessary.

A like situation obtains in the case of the mechanics of
the Christian life. If the Christian desires the highest degree of efficiency from the salvation which God has given
him, he must himself give special attention and care to his
personal adjustment to this machinery. The Christian who
is not informed as to the truth of Romans VI is in a position somewhat like the man who purchased a new automobile, but ignorant of the details of the mechanism, did
not bestow the proper care upon it. Soon only three out of
the six cylinders were operating. His car ran, but he was
not getting the maximum of power from it. The engine
stalled in traffic, became over-heated, and would not climb
hills in high gear. After he had learned the details of the

mechanism and had the parts properly adjusted, the engine gave him excellent service.

In the case of a Christian who does not understand Romans VI, the new spiritual mechanism which he received when he was saved, operates, but not at its highest efficiency. When he understands what Paul is teaching in verses 1-10, and puts into practice the directions relative to his adjustment to this new mechanism in verses 11-13, then he will be obtaining the highest degree of efficiency from it. And this is the explanation why some Christians are living such mediocre lives, while others are living Christlike lives. It is not that the child of God does not want to live the highest type of a Christian life. He does. If he fails, it is because he does not know how. Listen to Paul again, "To will is present with me; but how to perform that which is good I find not" (Rom. 7:18). This personal adjustment of the believer to his inner spiritual mechanism, Paul presents in verses 11-13.

The first responsibility of the believer is to reckon himself dead to sin. The word "reckon" is the translation of a Greek word meaning "to count, compute, calculate, take into account." That is, the believer is to live his Christian life upon the basis of the fact that the power of the sinful nature is broken. He is to take these facts into his reckoning as he deals with temptations that confront him or evil impulses that come from within. His attitude should be that, in view of the fact that the power of the evil nature is broken, he is under no obligation to obey its behests (Rom. 8:12). He has been emancipated from sin, and the proper procedure is to read God's emancipation proclamation to the insistent demands of the Adamic nature. The believer must also realize that whereas before salvation, he could not help it when he sinned, yet since God saved him, should he sin, it is because of his free choice, since sin's power has been broken. He is responsible for that sin. This should make him think twice before he contemplates an act of sin at the demand of the evil nature.

Then, he must also count upon the fact of his possession of the divine nature. This will keep him from depending upon himself and his own strength in his effort to live a life pleasing to the Lord Jesus, and will cause him to throw himself upon the resources of God. He will be trusting the Lord Jesus to fill him with the Holy Spirit (John 7:37, 38), with the result that the Holy Spirit will do two things for him. He will suppress the activities of the evil nature (Gal. 5:17) and He will produce in the believer a Christlike life (Gal. 5:22, 23). Paul says in Galations 5:16, 17, "This I say then, Walk in the Spirit, and ye shall not fulfill the cravings of the flesh, for the flesh has a strong desire to suppress the Spirit, and the Spirit has a strong desire to suppress the flesh, and these are entrenched in a permanent attitude of opposition to one another, so that ye should not do the things that ye would desire to be doing;" and in Galatians 5:22, 23, "The fruit of the Spirit is love, joy, peace, longsuffering, gentleness, goodness, faithfulness, meekness, self-control."

Contrast this adjustment of the intelligent Spirit-taught saint, with that of the believer who is not aware of the fact that God has broken the power of sin in his life, with the result that he is more or less under its compelling power, try as he may to live free from sin. Since he is ignorant of the fact that God has placed within him His own nature, he depends upon himself and his own strength in an effort to defeat sin in his life and live a life pleasing to God. This believer is living a defeated life because he is not in proper adjustment to the new mechanical set-up in his spiritual being. When he learns of the facts which Paul presents in verses 1-10, he has in his possession a knowledge of the scriptural method of gaining victory over sin and the living of a life pleasing to God, and, acting upon instructions which he finds in verses 11-13 he has victory all along the line. The translation of verse 11 follows: "Thus also, as for you, constantly be taking into account the fact that you are those who are dead with respect to sin, and indeed those who are living ones with reference to God in Christ Jesus." A paraphrase may make things clearer yet. "Thus also, as for you, constantly be taking into account the fact that you are those who have had the power of sin broken in your lives and those who have had the divine nature implanted."

We come to verse 12. The words "let not sin reign," are in a construction in the Greek which forbids the continuation of an action already going on. The word "reign" is in the Greek "reign as king." The tense speaks of habitual action. "That ye should obey" is literally, "with a view to habitually obeying." The word "lusts" is literally "cravings." "Thereof" does not go back to "sin" but to "body." The gender of the pronoun requires this. "Lusts thereof" refers to the cravings of the human body, which cravings come from the sinful nature. The translation reads, "Therefore, stop allowing sin to reign habitually as king in your mortal bodies, with a view to your habitually obeying the cravings of that body." God is never unreasonable in His demands upon His own. What He asks of us is always within our ability to fulfill as we appropriate the divine resources of grace. Since the power of sin is broken and the divine nature is implanted, we are well able to keep sin from reigning in our lives.

In verse 13, Paul presents other exhortations to be obeyed upon the basis of what God has done for us as recorded in verse 11. "Yield" is from a Greek word which means "to put at the service of." Together with the word "neither," it forbids the continuance of an action already going on.

"Stop habitually putting your members at the service of,"
is the translation. Our members refer to our hands, feet,
tongue, eyes, mind, for instance. The word "instruments"
is in the Greek, "weapons of warfare." The second use of
the word "yield" is in a tense different from that used in the
first occurrence of the word. The first time it is used in this
verse, it refers to habitual action, the second time, to an
act performed once for all. The translation reads, "Neither
keep on putting your members habitually at the service of
sin as weapons of unrighteousness, but put yourselves once
for all at the service of God as those who are living ones out
from among the dead, and put your members once for all
at the service of God as weapons of righteousness."

The Christian therefore never acts alone. He either acts
in the energy imparted by the evil nature, or in that imparted by the divine nature. He makes the choice. He need
not choose to obey the evil nature, for its power over him
is broken. The inclination of his power of choice is on the
side of the divine nature. As a child of God, his choices
naturally gravitate towards the latter. His responsibility is
to see that he keeps his power of choice in that direction.
Gradually, just as a tree bends with the prevailing winds,
so the will of a child of God bends more and more habitually and even automatically towards the divine nature and
the doing of the right and away from the doing of what is
wrong. That is what Paul refers to when he speaks of "the
good fight of faith." It is a constant battle to keep our
choices in the direction of the right and our faith in the
Lord Jesus for the divine enablement by which we are able
to do the right.

When we do this, we have God's promise that then sin
shall not have dominion over us: for we are not under law
but under grace. There is no article before "law" in the
original. We saints are not under law as an unsaved person

is with the obligation to obey a commandment which gives neither the desire nor the power for obedience. We are under grace, which sweetly exhorts to a holy life, and gives both the desire and the power necessary to live that life.

We come now to the second question, "What then? shall we sin, because we are not under the law but under grace?" It is the reaction to Paul's statement in 6:14, "Ye are not under the law, but under grace." But there is a difference in the way these two questions are put. In the first, the Greek text tells us that a life of habitual sin is referred to. In the second, the Greek tense indicates that occasional, infrequent, single acts of sin are spoken of. The thought in the speaker's mind is, "Since your doctrine of superabundant grace teaches the impossibility of a life of habitual sin on the part of the Christian, will the fact that a Christian is not under the uncompromising rule of law but under the lenient sceptre of grace, allow for at least an act of sin once in awhile?" The idea that grace is lenient as over against the uncompromising rule of law, is an erroneous one. The Holy Spirit dwelling in the heart of a child of God, is infinitely more cognizant of sin in the life of the saint than any system of law ever could be. He is grieved at the slightest sin. In the first question, the desperately wicked heart offers an excuse for sinning in that a life of habitual sin gives God an opportunity to display His grace and thus glorify Himself, which is of course a perversion of the teaching of grace. In the second question, this same person seeks a loophole somewhere in God's plan of salvation whereby he might sin once in awhile, and thinks that he has found one in the fact that the Christian is beyond the reach of the law of God which could condemn him. Therefore, he argues that he can sin with impunity, and grace will always forgive.

One can see at once from what Paul tells us in 6:1-14, that the person who asks such a question as well as the one

in 6:1, is an unregenerate sinner. O child of God has no desire to go on in habitual sin nor yet to sin once in awhile.
A Christian is at time guilty of wilful sin. That is, he may
yield to temptation, knowing that it is sin. But to provide
for a planned life of infrequent acts of sin, is altogether
foreign to the nature of the saint. Paul answers this question as he did the first one, by the words "God forbid," "far
be the thought." Then he uses an illustration to show that
it is a mechanical impossibility for a Christian to desire to
sin even once in awhile. The question is "What then? shall
we commit occasional acts of sin (as opposed to a life of
habitual sin) because we are not under law but under
grace?" The definite article does not appear before "law"
in the original. Law as a method of divine dealing is referred to.

Paul's second answer is, "Do ye not know that to whom
ye keep presenting yourselves for service as bondslaves resulting in your obedience (to that person), bondslaves ye
are to the one whom ye are obeying, whether it be bondslaves of sin resulting in death, or bondslaves of obedience
resulting in righteousness?" The word "servants" in the
A. V. does not adequately translate the full content of the
Greek word which Paul used. His first century reader understood the various implications of the word and therefore understood Paul's argument better.

In the first place, there are various Greek words which
refer to a slave. One speaks of a slave captured in war. Another refers to a person born into slavery. The latter word
is used here. The sinner by his first birth comes into this
world with a totally depraved nature which he inherited
through this first birth. This makes him a bondslave of
Satan, for this fallen nature causes him to love sin. When
he is born from above through the supernatural work of
the Holy Spirit in answer to his faith in the Lord Jesus as

his Saviour, he is given the divine nature which causes him to love the things of God, and thus he becomes a bondslave of Jesus Christ. Paul argues that because the believer has had his slavery transferred from one master to another, in that he has been given a nature that causes him to forsake his former master Satan and cleave to his new Master, the Lord Jesus, that it is both unreasonable and impossible for him to desire to serve his old master any more, even on infrequent occasions.

Another implication which the word had in the first century was that the slave is one bound to his master. The Christian before salvation, was bound to Satan by the shackles of sin. In his identification with Christ in His death, these shackles were stricken off, and in his participation with Christ in His resurrection, he was bound to his new Master, Christ. It is the nature of a slave to serve the master to whom he is bound, Paul argues. Thus, it is the nature of the Christian to serve Jesus Christ.

The word spoke of the slave as one whose will is swallowed up in the will of his master. Before salvation wrought its work in the believer, his will was swallowed up in the will of Satan (Eph. 2:1-3). His totally depraved nature bent his will always in that direction. But since God in salvation broke the power of that evil nature and thus released the believer's will from the control of the evil nature, and gave the believer the divine nature which at once inclined that liberated will toward God, the Christian's will is swallowed up in the sweet will of God. How unreasonable it is, Paul argues, to think that a Christian would want to sin even occasionally.

Again, the word referred to a slave who is devoted to the interests of his master to the extent that he disregards his own interests. Before salvation, the believer served Satan recklessly, and to the disregard of his own interests. All he

received for his slavery was death. But now his slavery has
been transferred. He serves Jesus Christ, his new Master,
not counting the cost to himself. Do you think, Paul argues, that a bondslave who loves his Lord and Master that
much, would presume upon His grace, and desire to commit an occasional act of sin? Paul argues therefore in verse
16 that to suggest that a child of God desires to commit an
occasional sin, would necessitate his becoming a slave of
Satan again, which is an impossibility since that would in-
volve a change of nature brought about by his loss of the
divine nature and his acquisition of the Adamic nature
again. Because the divine nature is the eternal possession
of the believer, and the Adamic nature could only be his
through natural generation, it is impossible, Paul answers,
for a believer to become a slave of Satan again, and therefore it is not possible for him to make provision for occasional acts of sin in his life.

And so Paul says in view of all this, "But God be
thanked that ye were (but are not now) by nature bondslaves of sin, but ye obeyed from your heart that type of
teaching to which ye were delivered." The definite article
does not appear before "servants" in verse 17. The absence
of the article qualifies. Emphasis is upon character, quality,
or nature. Thus we translated, "by nature bondslaves of
sin." That is, the quality or nature of the person made him
a bondslave of sin. Regarding the translation "that type
of teaching to which ye were delivered," we might say that
while Paul's teaching to which he here refers, was given the
Christians and thus could be said to have been delivered
to them, yet the Greek verb here is passive, and speaks of
the believer being delivered to the teaching. That is, Christians are so constituted that they naturally desire to obey
the Word of God. They have in salvation been handed over
to its obedience. Therefore, a child of God does not make

provision for occasional acts of sin, since he has ceased being a slave of Satan, and he has been so constituted inwardly by God that he renders obedience from the heart, willingly, to the Word of God. Paul adds this word of explanation to what he said in verse 17, "Having been set free from sin, ye became slaves of righteousness."

Now, after having explained that the thought of occasional sin in the life of a child of God is not to be entertained for a moment, because the believer's slavery has been transferred from one master, Satan, to another Master, even the Lord Jesus, and this, because the believer has had the power of the indwelling sinful nature broken and the divine nature implanted, Paul proceeds to show the attitude which the believer should be careful to maintain with reference to his change of masters. Paul apologizes for using such a human illustration as slavery to explain one's former relationship to Satan and one's present relationship to God. But he says that he finds it necessary to do so because of their defective spiritual insight which in turn is due to certain moral defects. The translation reads: "I am using a human term of speech because of the weakness of your flesh, for even as ye put your members as slaves at the service of uncleanness and lawlessness resulting in an abiding state of lawlessness, so now put your members once for all as slaves at the service of righteousness resulting in holiness."

One might ask at this point, why such an exhortation is necessary if the power of the evil nature has been broken and the divine nature implanted, resulting in a transfer of affection to another Master, even the Lord Jesus? Why is it necessary for Paul to exhort believers to put themselves at the service of Christ, when they have a nature that impels them to do so? The answer is that the will of the believer, even though it is inclined in regeneration towards Christ and the doing of good, still has a certain bent at times to the doing of evil, the result of the habitual and constant inclination it had towards evil before grace did its work. The habits formed by years of sin must be overcome. That moral twist must be unbent. *The only way to do this is to form new habits of the will by keeping our choices inclined towards obedience to our new Master, Christ. The divine nature is there to keep our choices in line with the Word of God as we yield to the ministry of the Holy Spirit and trust Him to work in us, but we must ever be on the alert lest those habits formed by years of choosing the wrong, lead us to render obedience to our old master, Satan. As we establish new habits of choice, gradually our renewed wills are bent more and more in the direction of the good, and it becomes increasingly easier to do the right and increasingly harder to do the wrong.*

Then Paul reminds the believer of the wasted years spent in sin, with their evil consequences. "For when ye were slaves of sin, ye were free with respect to righteousness." That is, in our unsaved state, there was no restraint put upon sin in our lives by any righteousness we might have had, for we had none. And because there was no check upon sin that would restrain evil in our lives, sin ran rampant. The apostle reminds the believer: "Therefore what fruit were ye constantly having at that time? of which things now ye are ashamed? for the end of those things is death." Thus another reason is presented why the believer does not want even to provide for an occasional sin in his life. He is ashamed of the years which he spent in sin, and of the corruption it bred. And so Paul concludes his argument with the words: "But now having been made free from sin and having become bondslaves of God, ye are having your fruit resulting in holiness, and the end, eternal life. For the pay which sin doles out is death, but the free gift of God is life eternal in Jesus Christ our Lord."

Thus Paul answers the second question: "What then? shall we sin occasionally because we are not under law but under grace?" by asserting that that cannot be the desire of a child of God and cannot be a fact in his life, and for the reason that he has had his slavery transferred from Satan to the Lord Jesus, this act of transference having been accomplished by the breaking of the power of the evil nature, which nature caused the person to love to serve the Devil, and by the impartation of the divine nature which impels the believer to serve the Lord Jesus.

Thus God's grace not only justifies the believer, that is, takes away the guilt and penalty of sin and bestows a positive righteousness, even the Lord Jesus Himself in whom the believer stands perfectly righteous for time and eternity, but it sanctifies him, in that it breaks the power of sin in his life, and produces in him a life which glorifies God.

Dear Christian reader, if you have not been obtaining consistent victory over sin, will you not let this study of Romans VI point the way to the victorious life? There is victory for you when you understand and follow God's directions with regard to the correct technique of how to gain this victory.

XV.

How To Be Hungry

PETER is speaking in his first epistle (2:1-3) of the divine imperative which must be obeyed if we as Christians expect to have a real hunger for God's Word. The words "laying aside" are in the Greek, not a command, but a past once-for-all action. The idea is, "having laid aside once for all." It is the God-expected action of every believer. Until he has made a complete break with all sin in his life, he cannot expect to have a hunger for the Word of God. The reason for this is that he has filled his heart with the husks of the world. This not only destroys his appetite but perverts his taste. Peter here gives us the reason why so many children of God have so little hunger for the Word.

The Greek word translated "guile" means "to catch with bait." We are not to be crafty, sly, underhanded persons, but above-board, open, sincere, accomplishing our purposes by fair means. "Hypocrisies" is from a Greek word used in the first century of one who impersonates another. How we saints sometimes play the part of something that we are not. Our faces should be open, free from deception, shining with the beauty of the Lord Jesus. A mask of deception hides Him. "Evil speakings" is literally, "speaking down" another person, that is, slandering him. The words "as new-born babes," describe the spiritual status of those to whom Peter is writing. The idea is, "as just-born babes, they should have an intense hunger for the Word of God."

The word "desire" is emphatic in the Greek, referring to an intense desire.

"Sincere" is from the Greek word for "guile," with the Greek letter Alpha prefixed, which negates its meaning. The idea is "unadulterated." God's Word is not like so many human teachings, adulterated with some ulterior motive, but pure, unadulterated, its only purpose that of blessing the one who puts his faith in it. The words "of the word" are from an adjective in the Greek, meaning literally "spiritual." "Grow" is literally, "be nourished up." The best Greek texts add to verse two the words, "and thus make progress in your salvation."

"If so be," does not imply a doubt but a fulfilled condition. These saints had found the Lord gracious. The word "gracious" is from a Greek word found also in Luke 5:39 where it is translated "better." Literally it means "excellent."

The translation reads: "Therefore, now that you have laid aside once for all every kind of wickedness and every kind of trickery, also hypocrisies, and envies, and all kinds of slanders, as just born infants, long for with an intense yearning the spiritual unadulterated milk, in order that by it you might be nourished up and thus make progress in your salvation, in view of the fact that you tasted for yourselves and have found that the Lord is excellent."

Sin in the life destroys one's appetite for the Word of God. When sin is put away, the normal thing is an intense hunger for the Word. The result is that we feed our souls upon it and thus make progress in our salvation.

XVI.

The Four-Fold Basis of Christian Unity

THE exhortations in the Pauline epistles grew out of the conditions found in the churches to which they were addressed. Because fallen human nature has not changed in two thousand years, conditions that obtained during Paul's time are existent in the churches of today.

There were minor divisions in the Philippian church, that church which in such a marked way helped in Paul's support as a missionary. Two of these divisions centered about two women in the church who were capable and prominent leaders in its work, especially taking leadership in supporting Paul. These women led two factions which were at variance with one another. To bring them together would be to heal the breach, not only between them, but between those who followed them.

The exhortation in Philippians 4:2, 3, is not abrupt. Paul had prepared the way by laying a groundwork for it in 2:1-4, where we have detailed exhortation, and 2:5-8, where we have the great Example portrayed who in His life exemplified the one outstanding thing that will heal all such divisions in the local church, namely, a Christlike humility. In 2:1, Paul presents four things which constitute the basis for unity among the saints. These demand careful treatment in the original.

First of all, the word "if" does not present a doubt as to whether there is any consolation in Christ. The word in the Greek presents a fulfilled condition, a fact, not a hypothetical case. For instance, a person says, "If it rains tomorrow, I shall carry an umbrella." That is, "It looks like it may rain. If it does, then I shall be prepared." This "if" introduces a guess, something possible in the future. But the "if" Paul uses is: "You say that he is preaching the gospel? Well, if he is doing that, the Lord will certainly bless him." The word could be translated, "since," or "in view of the fact." It represents a fulfilled condition. Paul is therefore exhorting to unity among the saints in the Philippian church in view of the fact that certain things are facts.

The first fact he presents is that there is a certain consolation in Christ. The word "any" in our translation is from a Greek word which is used with nouns of persons or things concerning which the writer cannot or will not speak particularly. The word "certain" is a good rendering. "Consolation" is from a word which does not mean "to console" in the sense of giving comfort. What these Philippian saints needed was not consolation, but exhortation. And "exhortation" is exactly what the word means. This exhortation to unity is found in Christ. His beautiful life is itself the exhortation to unity which these saints needed. His humility as spoken of in 2:5-8, is the very thing that would lead to unity, since the basis of these divisions was pride. His life therefore was the ground of appeal which Paul used. "In view of the fact that there is a certain ground of appeal in Christ which exhorts you, . . . be likeminded." If all the saints would keep their eyes on the Lord Jesus, and walk in His footsteps of humility, divisions in a local church would cease.

The second reason why there should be unity among the saints is that there is a "certain comfort of love." The word "comfort" comes from a Greek word made up of the words "beside," and "word," the entire word meaning "a word which comes to the side of one to stimulate or comfort." It speaks of persuasive address. It could be translated by the words, "incentive," or "encouragement." The word has the added element of tenderness in it.

The word "love" is from the Greek word for "divine love," the love that God is, the love which He produces in the heart of the saint wholly given over to the ministry of the Holy Spirit. The grammatical construction in the Greek makes it clear that this incentive to unity is produced by love. That is, the love which the Holy Spirit produces in the heart of the saint, causes and enables that saint to love his fellow-saint, and where divine love is, there is unity. Thus, love produces the incentive to unity. If the saints in a local church would love each other with the self-sacrificial love of John 3:16, and the love as analyzed for us in I Corinthians 13, divisions would cease, and unity would prevail. The secret of the possession of this love is found in a desire for the fullness of the Holy Spirit, and a trust in the Lord Jesus for that fullness (John 7:37, 38).

The third reason why unity should prevail among the saints is that there is a "certain fellowship of the Spirit." This does not mean that there is a fellowship between the saint and the Holy Spirit. The fellowship of the saint is with the Father and with His Son Jesus Christ (I John 1:3; Eph. 3:16, 17) made possible through the ministry of the Holy Spirit. The word "fellowship" is from a Greek word which refers to a relation between individuals which involves a common interest and a mutual, active participation in that interest. Here it refers to the ministry of the Spirit in the life of the saint, and the cooperation of the saint with the Spirit in His work of causing him to grow in grace, this cooperation consisting of the saint's yieldedness to the Spirit and the act of his free will in choosing the right and doing it. This ministry of the Spirit enables the saint to live in unity with his fellow-saints.

The fourth reason why the saints should be likeminded is that there are "certain bowels and mercies." In the orient, they speak of the heart, lungs, and liver as the seat of the tenderer affections. The word is translated "bowels." The Greek language has another word for the intestines. This word "bowels" is used in the east as we use the word "heart." "Mercies" is from a word which literally means "compassionate yearnings and actions." When brethren in the Lord are tenderhearted toward one another, and have compassion upon one another, divisions will cease and unity will prevail.

The four things therefore which will make for unity in a local church are, first, the exhortation which our Lord's life provides, namely, that of a Christlike humility, second, the incentive to unity which divine love provides as this love is produced in the heart of the saint by the Holy Spirit, third, the fact that each saint possesses the indwelling Holy Spirit who if yielded to will control that saint, and fourth, the fact that if saints show tenderheartedness to and compassion for each other, unity will prevail.

The fuller translation is as follows: In view of the fact therefore that there is a certain ground of appeal in Christ which exhorts, in view of the fact that there is a certain tender incentive which is produced by love, in view of the fact that there is a certain joint-participation with the Spirit in a common interest and activity, in view of the fact that there are certain tenderheartednesses and compassionate yearnings, fill full my joy by thinking the same thing, by having the same love, by being in heart-agreement, by thinking the one thing.

XVII.

The Meaning of "PERFECT" in the New Testament

THE Greek New Testament is the indispensable authority in cases where a wrong interpretation is put upon a
word in a translation. The word "perfect" is frequently
used in the meaning of "sinless." The easiest and most satis-
factory way to settle the question of the meaning of this
word when it is found in the New Testament, is to inquire
into the usage of the Greek word of which it is the translation.

Moulton and Milligan in their *Vocabulary of the Greek
Testament* which is based upon a study of the secular manuscripts using the same kind of Greek found in the New
Testament, give the following uses of the word *teleios,*
which is the word translated "perfect." It is found in the
phrases "to her heirs being *of age;* all proving that women
who have attained *maturity* are mistresses of their persons
and can remain with their husbands or not as they choose;
four *full-grown* cocks;" the italicised words being the translation of the Greek word *teleios.* From these illustrations
of its use, we would define the word as meaning "full-grown
mature." They report these instances also; "fourteen acacia
trees in *good condition;* four cocks in *perfect condition;*
a *complete* lampstand; in *good working order or condition;*
one *perfect* Theban mill." In the case of the chickens it
means "soundness, freedom from sickness and physical de-
fect." In the case of the mill, it describes it as being in good

working order and condition, that is, in such condition that the desired results would be obtained when it is operated. In the case of the lampstand, it speaks of the fact that all necessary parts are included. To summarize; the meaning of the word includes the ideas of "full-growth, maturity, workability, soundness, and completeness." In the pagan Greek mystery religions, the word referred to those devotees who were fully instructed as opposed to those who were novices.

Thayer in his *Lexicon of the Greek New Testament* gives the following meanings; *brought to its end, finished, wanting nothing necessary to completeness;* when used of men it means *full-grown, adult, of full age, mature.*

Now, we will look at some instances where Paul uses this Greek word in a context which defines it by contrast with another word. The words "full age" (Heb. 5:14) are from *teleios* which is set in contrast to the word "babe" (Heb. 5:13). The word "babe" is from *nepios,* a Greek word meaning "an infant, a little child, a minor, not of age," and in a metaphorical sense, "untaught, unskilled." The idea of immaturity is in the word, and according to the context in which it is found, it could refer to either mental or spiritual immaturity. Paul defines the word when he says that the person whom he calls a babe is "unskillful in the word of righteousness." Spiritual immaturity is referred to by the word "babe." Thus those spoken of as of full age are spiritually mature. The word *teleios* therefore when used of a Christian, describes him as spiritually mature.

Paul writes the Corinthians that he speaks wisdom among those who are perfect (I Cor. 2:6), and uses *teleios*. But he says that he could not speak to them as to spiritual Christians, but as to carnal ones, namely, babes in Christ (I Cor. 3:1). In passing, it might be well to note that the phrase "babes in Christ" as Paul uses it in the Greek, does not mean "young converts," but "Christians who have not attained to a mature Christian experience." It is a sad thing to see one who has been a Christian for many years and who is still a babe in Christ, immature. Here we have the same contrast which we found in the Hebrew passage, between *teleios* "perfect," that is, mature, and *nepios*, "babe," immature. Paul makes it clear that he is speaking of maturity and immaturity in spiritual things when he uses the word "spiritual" in 3:1 as describing the person in 2:6 who was spoken of as "perfect." Thus, the word "perfect" when used to describe a Christian means "spiritually mature."

In Ephesians 4:13, 14, we have the same contrast between a perfect (*teleios*) man and children (*nepios*). But *teleios* has an added shade of meaning here. Not only does it refer to spiritual maturity by its contrast to *nepios* which speaks of spiritual immaturity, but it speaks also of completeness. This latter shade of meaning comes from the words in the context, "the measure of the stature of the fulness of Christ." The word "completeness" speaks of a well-rounded Christian character, where the Christian graces are kept in proper balance. For instance, a Christian who has much zeal but little wisdom to guide that zeal into its proper channels and restrain it when necessary, is not a well balanced Christian, and not spiritually mature.

We come now to Paul's use of *teleios* and the verb of the same root *teleioo* in Philippians 3:12-15, which passage in the English translation (Authorized Version) involves a contradiction because the meaning of the tense of the verb could not be fully and clearly brought out in a translation such as the Authorized which is held down to a minimum of words. In 3:12, Paul states that he is not yet perfect. In 3:15, he urges those of the Philippian saints who are perfect to be "thus minded," namely, to account themselves as not yet perfect. How are we to understand this? Surely, the inspired Apostle does not ask them to deny the reality of something which they know to be a fact. The Greek solves the difficulty presented in the English.

The words "were already perfect" are from a word meaning "already" and the verb *teleioo* which means "to bring to the state of spiritual maturity." This verb is in the perfect tense which speaks of an action that was completed in past time, having results that exist in present time. The past completed action of this verb would refer to the process of sanctification, namely, the work of the Holy Spirit bringing the saint to that place of spiritual maturity in which the sanctifying process would have done its work so well that nothing needed to be added. In other words, the saint would be brought to a place of absolute spiritual maturity beyond which there is no room for growth. Furthermore, the results of this work would be permanent, and there would be no possibility of slipping back into a state of spiritual immaturity again. All this is involved in Paul's use of this tense. That Paul deliberately used this tense is clearly seen from the fact that the tense he used in the previous verb is the aorist, which is the customary tense used by the Greek when he desires merely to refer to a fact without referring to details. Whenever a Greek uses any other tense, he goes out of his way to do so. It is a sign that he wishes to refer to that fact in detail and for a certain purpose. When Paul says, "Not as though I . . . were already perfect," he means that the Holy Spirit had not yet brought him to the place in his Christian life where His sanctifying work was no longer needed, in other words, to the place of absolute spiritual maturity from which place there was no possibility of slipping back to a condition of spiritual immaturity, and beyond which there was no room for growth.

Then he exhorts those among the Philippian saints who were spiritually mature, to take the same attitude towards their own growth in grace. And here he uses the word *teleios* in a noun form, and in a relative sense. That is, a Christian is spiritually mature if he is not *nepios,* a babe. Just as an adult becomes more mature as he grows older and wiser, so a child of God grows in degrees of spiritual maturity. But he must ever realize that he will never be spiritually mature in an absolute sense, that is, come to the place where he cannot grow in the Christian life. He must always realize how far short he comes of absolute Christlikeness, what an infinite distance there is between the most Christlike saint and the Lord Jesus.

Thus, the contradiction in the English translation is cleared up by the Greek text. In 3:12, Paul is speaking of absolute spiritual maturity, in 3:15, of relative spiritual maturity. In 3:12, he is speaking of a process that had reached a state of completion. In 3:15, he refers to a process that was still going on. In 3:12, he denies having reached the place in his Christian life where there was no more improvement possible. In 3:15, he speaks of the constant need of growth in the Christian life. In 3:12 he denies being spiritually mature in an absolute sense. In 3:15, he asserts that as a spiritually mature Christian, he sees a need of more maturity in his spiritual experience.

It remains for us to trace briefly the use of *teleios* in the other passages where it occurs. In Matthew 5:48, the word implies growth into maturity of godliness on the part of the believer. The word when used here of God the Father does not refer to His sinlessness, but to His kindness, as the context points out, thus to His character. In Matthew 19:21, that spiritual maturity is meant which is the result and accompaniment of a self-sacrificial character. In Romans 12:2, it describes the will of God as a will that lacks nothing necessary to completeness. In I Corinthians 13:10, the word means "complete," and is contrasted to that which is incomplete. In I Corinthians 14:20, "be ye children," is from our word *nepios* which means "immaturity," while "men" is our word *teleios*, which here speaks of spiritual maturity. In Colossians 1:28, Paul's desire is to present the saints to whom he ministers as spiritually mature believers. Epaphras (Col. 4:12) prays that the Colossian saints might be spiritually mature believers. In Hebrews 9:11, the tabernacle of the New Testament in heaven is said to be more complete than the tabernacle which Moses built, for the latter lacked what the former has, the out-poured blood of Christ.

In James 1:4, 17, 25, *teleios* means "wanting nothing to completeness." In 3:2, it speaks of spiritual maturity. In I John 4:18 we have, "love that is wanting nothing necessary to completeness, casteth out fear." We have treated every occurrence of the word *teleios* in the New Testament. There are two places where *teleiotes* is used. In Colossians 3:12-14, the believer is exhorted to put on the Christian graces mentioned, as one puts on a garment. Then over all these he is put on charity (love, God's love supplied by the Holy Spirit, Gal. 5:22). The word "which" does not go back to "love," as the Greek indicates, but refers to the act of "putting on." That is, the act of putting on love as a garment over these other virtues, completes and keeps together all the rest, which, without it, are but the scattered elements of *teleiotes*, "perfectness" or "completeness." These other virtues are manifestations of love, but may be exhibited where love is absent. They are worthwhile only when permeated with divine love. Thus, this putting on of love makes for perfection in the sense of completeness of Christian character. Love is the binding factor which binds together our Christian garments as would a girdle. In Hebrews 6:1, this word refers to that which is complete, wanting nothing necessary to completeness, here the New Testament as contrasted to the incomplete First Testament consisting of animal sacrifices.

It remains for us to look at the places where the word "perfect" appears in the translation of the verb *teleioo*. In Luke 13:32, "today, tomorrow and the third day" is an expression used to designate a short while. "Perfected" here is used in the same sense as in Hebrews 2:10. In His death on the Cross, Jesus was made complete as the Saviour. In John 17:23 "made perfect" is to be understood in the sense of "brought to a state of completeness." The word "one" refers to the unity into which believers are brought by the fact that the Lord Jesus is in each saint. In being united together by the indwelling Christ, believers are in that state of completeness with reference to their salvation which would not be true of them if Christ were not in them. In II Corinthians 12:9, Paul's strength is brought to such a state by the power of the Holy Spirit that it is lacking nothing necessary to completeness. In Hebrews 2:10 and 5:9, the Lord Jesus through His death on the Cross was made perfect in that He was made complete as a Saviour; in 7:19 the Mosaic economy brought nothing to completeness in that it could not offer a sacrifice that could pay for sin. In Hebrews 9:9 and 10:1, we are told that the Levitical sacrifices could not make believers perfect, while in 10:14 and 12:23, we find that the New Testament sealed in Jesus' blood does.

In Hebrews 9:9, "make perfect as pertaining to the conscience," refers to the inability of the typical sacrifices themselves to bring the believer's conscience to a state of completeness in the sense that they could not "put his moral-religious consciousness in its inward feeling into a state of entire and joyful looking for of salvation so that his conscience should be an onward-waxing consciousness of perfect restoration, of entire clearing up, of total emancipation, of his relation to God" (Alford). The words "make perfect as pertaining to the conscience," therefore, refer to that work of God in salvation that is a complete work in the believer's conscience. "Abraham rejoiced to see my day," means that he rejoiced to see in the future of God's prophetic program, the death and resurrection of Messiah. The very fact of the constant repetition of the sacrifices showed him that sin had not yet been actually paid for. Thus believers under the First Testament sacrifices never had that sense of completeness in which there was nothing lacking that was necessary (Heb. 10:1). But our Lord on the Cross cried, "It stands completed," using the word *teleioo,* referring to His work of salvation wrought out on the Cross (John 19:30). Thus, believers today have that complete sense of forgiveness which was lacking in the Old Testament saints (Heb. 10:14). Abraham had righteousness reckoned to him, that is, put to his account. But he did not possess it as the believer does today. Therefore, he was not as complete in salvation as we are. He received that righteousness actually in his identification with Christ in His resurrection.

In Hebrews 12:23 we have "the spirits of just men made perfect." The Greek shows that it is the men who are made perfect. These are saints in heaven, made perfect in the sense that they have been brought to that spiritual maturity which is the result of sufferings, trials, of having run and ended their race. "All is accomplished, their probation, their righteousness, God's purposes respecting them." There is a completeness about them that is lacking in the saints yet on earth.

In James 2:22, Abraham's works made his faith perfect in the sense that it made that faith a complete faith. There is an intellectual assent which is not a complete saving faith (James 2:19). But in order for faith to issue in good works, it must be a faith that is the heart's submission to God. Abraham's obedience to God in preparing to sacrifice his son Isaac, drew out of his heart a faith that submitted to God's will. Thus his faith was made complete, lacking nothing necessary to a state of completeness. In I John 2:5 we have "in him verily is the love of God brought to a state of completeness." The word has the same meaning in 4:12, 17. In 4:18 we translate, "He that feareth is not brought to the state of spiritual maturity in the sphere of love."

XVIII.

About Anointing

THERE are two Greek words, both meaning "to anoint," and as used in the New Testament, referring to different kinds of anointing, and for different purposes. These are translated by the one English word "anoint." In order to arrive at a full-orbed accurate interpretation of the passages in which the word "anoint" occurs, it is necessary to know what Greek word lies back of the English translation.

One word is *aleipho*. The non-literary manuscripts of the early centuries give us some instances of its use as seen in the following examples: "which you will carefully grease," spoken of a yoke-band; a man whose wife had gone away, writes to her that since they had bathed together a month before, he had never bathed or anointed himself; an inscription in honor of a gymnasiarch, namely, the head of a gymnasium, does him honor as the "much-honored anointer." In the first case, the word is used of the action of applying grease to the yoke-band, the purpose of which was to keep it from chafing the ox. In the other two instances, it referred to the practice, common in the orient, of giving the body an olive-oil massage. Olive-oil was used in the east for medicinal and remedial purposes in the case of illness. It provided an excellent rub-down for the tired athlete after exercise. It prevented skin dryness in the hot dry climate of the orient.

We see this use of the word *aleipho* in Mark 6:13 and James 5:14, where the word is used of the application of oil for medicinal purposes. Thus we find in the latter text, the two God-appointed resources in the case of illness, prayer and medical help. It is also used of the application of ointment. A passage in Xenophon speaks of the greater suitableness of oil for the men and of ointment for women, saying that the latter are better pleased that the men should savour of the manly oil than the effeminate ointment. The ointment had oil for its base, but differed from the common oil in that it was highly scented. We can better understand the words of our Lord to the discourteous Pharisee (Luke 7:46), "My head with oil thou didst not anoint: but this woman hath anointed my feet with ointment." It was as if He said, "Thou withheldest from Me cheap and ordinary courtesies; while she bestowed upon Me costly and rare homages" (Trench). The Pharisee withheld from our Lord the courtesy of common oil for His head, that same anointing oil which the hypocrites denied themselves (Matt. 6:17). The woman anointed His tired, parched feet with the expensive, highly fragrant ointment which she as a woman naturally possessed, rather than with the anointing oil used commonly by men. The same precious ointment was used by Mary of Bethany (John 11:2, 12:3), and by the women at the tomb (Mark 16:1). How the fragrance of that ointment which permeated the room, spoke of the heavenly fragrance of the one Man among all men who combined in His wonderful Person and in most delicate balance, the gentleness of womanhood and the strength and virility of manhood, without either one detracting from the other. In the Septuagint, the Greek translation of the Old Testament, *aleipho* is the usual word for anointing with oil for either of the above purposes, although the other word for "anoint" is used in Amos 6:6. It is used in Ruth 3:3; II Samuel 12:20, 14:2; Daniel 10:3; Micah 6:15. *Aleipho* is the only word used for anointing with oil in the New Testament, there being no exceptions to this.

The other word used in the New Testament is *chrio*. It is never used here in connection with oil, but uniformly of the anointing with the Holy Spirit, although in the secular documents it had the same meaning as *aleipho*. *Chrio* is used in "The Spirit of the Lord is upon me, for he hath anointed me" (Luke 4:18), a quotation from Isaiah 61:1, where the same Greek word appears in the Septuagint translation. It is used in Acts 4:27, 10:38, of the anointing of our Lord with the Holy Spirit. In II Corinthians 1:21 the word is used in connection with the anointing of the believer with the Spirit. Hebrews 1:9 presents a seeming deviation of the rule that *chrio* is never used in the New Testament in connection with the anointing with oil. We have "God hath anointed thee (the Lord Jesus) with the oil of gladness," and *chrio* is used. How true the inspired writer was to the genius of the two words as they are used in the New Testament, for the word "oil" here does not refer to literal oil, but is symbolic of the Holy Spirit. In I John 2:20, 27, "unction" and "anointing" are from the noun form that comes from *chrio,* and refer to the anointing of the believer with the Holy Spirit.

Chrio is the usual word in the Septuagint of the anointing of the priests and kings at their induction into office. The anointing is with oil, but this oil is symbolic of the anointing of the Spirit, not for medicinal purposes. *Aleipho* is used in Exodus 40:15, which speaks of the anointing of the priest, and its usage here is an exception to the usual practice. The priest was anointed once only, at the time of his induction into the priest's office, the anointing being symbolic of a reality, the anointing with the Holy Spirit who by His presence with him, equipped the priest for his service. Believers in this Christian era are priests in the

New Testament sense. They are anointed with the Holy
Spirit once and once only, at the moment they are saved.
This anointing is the coming of the Spirit to take up His
permanent residence in their hearts, thus providing the po-
tential equipment for their service as priests. The baptism
by the Spirit is for the introduction of the believer into the
Body of Christ, the anointing with the Spirit is His coming
to dwell in the Christian, and the fullness of the Spirit is
for power for service.

XIX.

Two Kinds of Testings

THERE are two words in the Greek New Testament both meaning "to test." It is important in the interests of accurate interpretation, to distinguish between them, since they refer to different kinds of testings.

One is *dokimazo*. We will look at some instances of its use in the early manuscripts. These are of great help in the forming of an accurate judgment as to the usages of New Testament words, since an illustration is often clearer than a definition. The word is used in a manuscript of A.D. 140 which contains a plea for the exemption of physicians, and especially of those who have passed the examination. The words, "passed the examination" are the translation of *dokimazo*. From this we arrive at the definition. The word refers to the act of testing someone or something for the purpose of approving it. These physicians had passed their examinations for the degree of Doctor of Medicine. In the inscriptions, the word is almost a technical term for passing as fit for a public office. It is found in the sentence, "Whichever way, then, you also *approve* of, so it shall be," and in the phrase, "To instruct, if you will, the strategus or any other magistrate whom you may *sanction*."* The words "approve" and "sanction" are the translations of *dokimazo*.

The word has in it the idea of proving a thing whether it be worthy to be received or not. In classical Greek, it is

---

Moulton and Milligan.

the technical word for putting money to the test. In the New Testament almost always it implies that the proof is victoriously surmounted. The word further implies that the trial itself was made in the expectation and hope that the issue would be such. At all events, there was no contrary hope or expectation.

The other word is *peirazo*. The word meant in the first place "to pierce, search, attempt." Then it came to mean "to try or test intentionally, and with the purpose of discovering what good or evil, what power or weakness, was in a person or thing." But the fact that men so often break down under this test, gave *peirazo* a predominant sense of putting to the proof with the intention and the hope that the one put to the test may break down under the test. Thus the word is used constantly of the solicitations and suggestions of Satan.

Dokimazo is used generally of God, but never of Satan, for Satan never puts to the test in order that he may approve. *Peirazo* is used at times of God, but only in the sense of testing in order to discover what evil or good may be in a person.

The English reader can see from this study that it is important that one recognize the difference in these words which both mean "to test," especially when one learns that they have the same translation in some parts of the New Testament. For instance, *dokimazo* occurs in Luke 14:19 and *peirazo* in John 6:6, and yet the one English word "prove" is the translation. The man who bought the oxen went to examine them, not for the purpose of discovering what their good points might be or whether they had any defects. He bought them for sound, healthy stock, and fully expecting that they were what the seller represented them to be, he merely went to put his approval upon what he had bought. That is *dokimazo*. When our Lord propounded

the question to Philip, "Whence shall we buy bread, that
these may eat?" He was testing him to discover what faith
or lack of faith, what clear spiritual insight or lack of it,
what natural or supernatural view, that apostle might have.
The test brought out what was in Philip's thinking. He
was reasoning along a naturalistic plane. That is *peirazo*.
These two words are translated by the one English word
"try" in Revelation 2:2 and I Corinthians 3:13. At the
Judgment Seat of Christ, the believer's service will be tested, not for the purpose of finding out what good or evil
there was in it, but to put God's approval upon that part of
it which was the work of the Holy Spirit. A "Well done
thou good and faithful servant . . . enter thou into the joy
of thy Lord" (Matt. 25:23), and a reward in addition to
those blessed words, are awaiting every believer in the Lord
Jesus, for God will put His approval upon the Spirit-
wrought works of the saints and reward them. It is precious to note that *dokimazo* is used here, not *peirazo*. The
believer's works are not up for judgment with a penalty attached for those works not done in the power of the Holy
Spirit. These latter works will be burned up, and the believer will lose the reward he would have received had they
been done in the power of the Spirit. The Judgment Seat
of Christ is not for the judgment of the believer himself,
and certainly not for his retention or loss of salvation. It is
not *peirazo*, to discover what evil or good there may be. It
is *dokimazo*, to examine in order to approve. God expects
to find that in the service of the saint upon which He can
put His approval, for the Holy Spirit produces good works
in all the saints (Eph. 2:10), more in those who are definitely subjected to His control.

In the case of the Church at Ephesus (Rev. 2:2) "trying"
those who came to it representing themselves as apostles,
we have *peirazo*. The Church was suspicious of these stran-

gers. It had no reason to believe that it would find in these men that upon which it could put its approval. Thus *dokimazo* is not used here. The Church put these men to the test, that is, examined them to see what good or evil there was in them, intending to accept them if good, but to reject them if evil. They found them to be liars.

Both words are translated "examine" in I Corinthians 11:28 and II Corinthians 13:5. In the former passage, it is expected that the believer partake of the bread and wine at the Lord's table only when he can approve his life after having examined himself. If he finds nothing between him and his Saviour, then he is in an approved state, eligible to observe the Lord's Supper. This is *dokimazo*. In the second passage, the members of the Corinthian assembly are exhorted to examine themselves to see whether they are true believers or not. This is in accord with the meaning of *peirazo*, namely, that of finding out what there is of good or evil in a person. If the examination showed that they were true believers *peirazo*, then they could "prove" themselves, that is, put their approval upon that fact, the word "prove" being the translation of *dokimazo*. We will now list the places where each word is found, and study a few representative passages, leaving for the reader the delightful task of looking into the other instances of their use in the light of the distinctive meanings of each word.

Dokimazo is found in the following places and is translated by the words "discern, prove, did like, approve, try, examine, allow;" Luke 12:56, 14:19; Romans 1:28; 2:18, 12:2, 14:22; I Corinthians 3:13, 11:28, 16:3; II Corinhtians 8:8, 22, 13:5 ("prove"), Galatians 6:4; Ephesians 5:10; Philippians 1:10; I Thessalonians 2:4, 5:21; I Timothy 3:10; Hebrews 3:9; I Peter 1:7; I John 4:1. In Luke 12:56, the hypocrites could examine the weather conditions and put their approval upon them, but they were unable to understand the propitious character of the coming of Messiah to Israel, and then put their approval upon it. In Romans 1:28, lost humanity after scanning Deity for the purpose of putting its approval upon Him, did not find anything in or about Him that met with its approval, a sad commentary upon the total depravity of the human heart. In Romans 14:22 we have, "Spiritually prosperous is he who does not condemn himself in the thing which after having examined, he has put his approval upon." In I Thessalonians 2:4, Paul says that after God examined him, He put His approval upon him as one worthy to be entrusted with the gospel, the words "allowed" and "trieth" being from *dokimazo*. The other occurrences of *dokimazo* are translated by the words "prove, try, and examine," and the English reader should have no difficulty with them.

We come now to the places where *peirazo* is used, and where it is translated by the words "tempt, try, hath gone about, assayed." The word is found in Matthew 4:1, 3, 7, 16:1, 19:3, 22:18, 35; Mark 1:13, 8:11, 10:2, 12:15; Luke 4:2, 11:16, 20:23; John 6:6, 8:6; Acts 5:9, 15:10; 16:7, 24:6; I Corinthians 7:5, 10:9, 13; II Corinthians 13:5; Galatians 6:1; I Thessalonians 3:5; Hebrews 2:18, 3:9, 4:15, 11:17, 37; James 1:13, 14; Revelation 2:2, 10, 3:10. We will look at some representative passages. In Matthew 4:1, our Lord was led by the Holy Spirit into the wilderness to be tested by the Devil, the test being in the form of solicitations to do evil. In Matthew 4:7 our Lord said to Satan, "It stands written, Thou shalt not put the Lord thy God to the test" (to see what good or evil there may be in Him). The word does not mean here "to solicit to do evil." In Matthew 22:18, our Lord asks the hypocrites why they are putting Him to the test. Such an action on the part of man with relation to God always shows a state of unbelief. The words "hath gone about" in Acts 24:6 are from *peirazo*.

Paul was charged with bringing Greeks into the temple at Jerusalem, making a test-case of his action, possibly to show that Gentiles in this Age of Grace were not only admitted into salvation along with Israel, and were members of the same Body, but that they also had equal access to the Jewish temple along with the Jews. The charges of course were false, but they show the Jewish attitude towards Paul's ministry to the Gentiles. In I Corinthians 10:13, the word "tempted" refers to any test which Satan may put before us, the purpose of which is of course to bring out evil in our lives if he can, as in the case of Job, or a direct solicitation to do evil, as in the case of Israel as seen in the context. In Hebrews 11:17, Abraham when he was tried, that is, put to the test by God to see whether his faith would surmount the obstacle of the loss of his son, met the test, thus demonstrating his faith. The word *peirazo* is found in the Septuagint translation of the Old Testament passage reporting this incident, and is translated "tempted." In James 1:13, 14, the word "tempted" is to be understood as "solicit to do evil." God at times does test man in order to show man his sinfulness and develop his character (James 1:2, 12), but He never solicits man to do evil.

With the aid of this preliminary study, the student of the English Bible is equipped to study for himself in the light of the Greek text, all the texts in the New Testament using the words *dokimazo* and *peirazo*.

THE END

INDEX OF SCRIPTURE REFERENCES

	Page
Matthew 2:1-11	68
Matthew 3:7	86
Matthew 3:8	78
Matthew 3:11	74, 76, 77
Matthew 3:16	86
Matthew 4:1, 3, 7	130
Matthew 5:1-12	20
Matthew 5:22, 29, 30	44, 45
Matthew 5:48	117
Matthew 6:2	65
Matthew 6:17	123
Matthew 8:17	74
Matthew 8:26	72
Matthew 10:28	45
Matthew 11:23	46
Matthew 12:16	72
Matthew 12:22	48
Matthew 12:41	77
Matthew 16:1	130
Matthew 16:18	47
Matthew 16:22	72
Matthew 16:23	70
Matthew 17:18	72
Matthew 18:8	40
Matthew 18:9	45
Matthew 18:15	72
Matthew 19:3	130
Matthew 19:13	70, 72
Matthew 19:21	117
Matthew 20:12	74
Matthew 20:28	16
Matthew 20:31	72
Matthew 22:18, 35	130
Matthew 23:15, 33	45
Matthew 23:37-39	17
Matthew 25:23	128
Matthew 25:41	40, 41, 44
Matthew 25:43	61
Matthew 25:46	39, 40
Mark 1:7	74
Mark 1:13	130
Mark 1:25	72
Mark 3:12	72
Mark 3:29	40
Mark 4:39	72
Mark 6:13	123
Mark 7:4	86
Mark 8:11	130
Mark 8:30, 32, 33	72
Mark 9:25	70, 72
Mark 9:43, 45, 47	40, 45
Mark 10:2	130
Mark 10:13	72
Mark 10:17	38
Mark 10:30	38
Mark 10:48	72
Mark 12:15	130
Mark 14:13	74
Mark 16:1	123
Luke 1:33	37
Luke 1:55	37
Luke 1:68	62
Luke 1:78	62
Luke 2:11	32
Luke 3:19	72
Luke 4:2	130
Luke 4:18	124
Luke 4:22	16
Luke 4:35, 39, 41	72
Luke 5:39	108
Luke 7:14	74
Luke 7:16	62
Luke 7:46	123
Luke 8:24	72
Luke 9:21, 42, 55	72
Luke 10:15	46
Luke 10:25	38
Luke 11:16	130
Luke 12:5	45
Luke 12:56	129
Luke 13:32	119
Luke 14:19	127, 129
Luke 14:27	74
Luke 16:22	45

INDEX OF SCRIPTURE REFERENCES—Continued

	Page
Luke 16:23	46
Luke 16:24	86
Luke 17:3	72
Luke 17:9	17
Luke 18:15	72
Luke 18:18	38
Luke 18:30	38
Luke 18:39	70, 72
Luke 19:39	72
Luke 19:44	62
Luke 20:23	130
Luke 22:10	74
Luke 23:40	70, 72
Luke 23:43	45
Luke 23:46	46
John 1:1	76
John 2:17	16
John 3:3, 4	21
John 3:15	38
John 3:16	19, 38, 59
John 3:20	71, 72
John 3:36	38
John 4:1	86
John 4:13, 14, 36	29, 38
John 5:24, 39	38
John 6:6	127, 130
John 6:27	38
John 6:37	26
John 6:40	38
John 6:47	38
John 6:51	28, 38
John 6:54	38
John 6:58	38
John 6:66	67
John 6:68	38
John 7:37, 38	22, 30
John 8:6	130
John 8:9	72
John 8:35	37
John 8:46	71, 72
John 8:51, 52	38, 48
John 10:27-30	28, 38
John 10:31	74
John 11:2	123
John 11:26	38
John 12:3	123
John 12:6	74
John 12:25	38
John 12:34	37
John 12:50	38
John 15:7	26
John 16:8	71, 72
John 16:12	74
John 17:2, 3	38
John 17:23	119
John 19:17	74
John 19:30	120
John 20:15	74
Acts 1:20	63
Acts 2:27, 31	46
Acts 2:38	76, 77
Acts 3:2	74
Acts 3:4	49
Acts 4:27	124
Acts 5:9	130
Acts 6:1	53
Acts 7:23	62
Acts 9:15	72
Acts 10:38	124
Acts 11:18	77
Acts 11:26	67
Acts 13:46, 48	38
Acts 15:10	74, 130
Acts 15:14	62
Acts 15:36	63
Acts 16:7	130
Acts 16:33	86
Acts 17:28	53
Acts 17:29	75
Acts 20:28	49, 63
Acts 21:35	74
Acts 22:3	53
Acts 24:6	130
Acts 26:	69
Romans 1:1	50
Romans 1:16	76
Romans 1:19	75
Romans 1:20	74, 75
Romans 1:25	37
Romans 1:28	129, 130

INDEX OF SCRIPTURE REFERENCES—Continued

Page

Romans 2:7 38
Romans 2:18 129
Romans 4:4, 5 18
Romans 4:20 77
Romans 5:7-10 .... 17, 18
Romans 5:20 ....18, 80
Romans 5:21 38
Romans 6:1-23 ..17, 38, 51, 79, 106
Romans 7:15 80
Romans 7:18, 21 ....82, 96
Romans 8:11 90
Romans 8:12 96
Romans 9:5 37
Romans 11:6 18
Romans 11:36 37
Romans 12:2 ......37, 117, 129
Romans 14:22 ....129, 130
Romans 15:1 74
Romans 15:6 32
Romans 16:25 37
Romans 16:26 ....37, 38
Romans 16:27 37
I Corinthians 1:14 86
I Corinthians 2:6 114
I Corinthians 2:14 80
I Corinthians 2:15 80
I Corinthians 3:1 ....80, 114
I Corinthians 3:13 .....128, 129
I Corinthians 6:20 51
I Corinthians 7:5 130
I Corinthians 7:22, 23 ...50, 51
I Corinthians 10:9, 13 ..130, 131
I Corinthians 11:28 129
I Corinthians 12:13 ......84, 87
I Corinthians 13: 59, 111, 117
I Corinthians 14:20 118
I Corinthians 14:24 72
I Corinthians 15:24 32
I Corinthians 15:55 ...... 46, 49
I Corinthians 16:3 129
II Corinthians 1:3 32
II Corinthians 1:21 124
II Corinthians 4:17, 18 38
II Corinthians 5:1 38
II Corinthians 8:8 129

Page

II Corinthians 8:16 17
II Corinthians 8:22 129
II Corinthians 11:31 ......32, 37
II Corinthians 12:4 45
II Corinthians 12:9 119
II Corinthians 13:5 ......129, 130
Galatians 1:4 32
Galatians 1:5 37
Galatians 3:13 51
Galatians 4:19 93
Galatians 5:10 74
Galatians 5:16, 17 .... 95, 97
Galatians 5:22, 23 ....60, 95, 97
Galatians 6:1 130
Galatians 6:2 74
Galatians 6:4 129
Galatians 6:5 74
Galatians 6:8 38
Galatians 6:17 ....73, 74
Ephesians 2:1-3 ....51, 102
Ephesians 2:10 128
Ephesians 3:11 37
Ephesians 3:16 17 111
Ephesians 4:11 31
Ephesians 4:13, 14 115
Ephesians 5:10 129
Ephesians 5:11, 13 72
Ephesians 5:20 32
Philippians 1:1 63
Philippians 1:3-5 55
Philippians 1:10 129
Philippians 1:21 93
Philippians 1:23 45
Philippians 2:1-4 109
Philippians 2:5-8 109
Philippians 2:11, 12 83
Philippians 3:12-15 115
Philippians 4:2, 3 109
Philippians 4:10-19 ....25, 56, 66
Philippians 4:20 ....32, 37
Colossians 1:13 87
Colossians 1:26 37
Colossians 1:27 93
Colossians 1:28 118
Colossians 2:9 75

INDEX OF SCRIPTURE REFERENCES—Continued

Page

Colossians 3:4 ....38, 92
Colossians 3:12-14 118
Colossians 4:12 118
I Thessalonians 1:3 32
I Thessalonians 2:4 .....129, 130
I Thessalonians 3:5 130
I Thessalonians 3:11, 13 32
I Thessalonians 4:14 49
I Thessalonians 5:21 129
II Thessalonians 1:9 41
II Thessalonians 3:11 66
I Timothy 1:16 38
I Timothy 1:17 37
I Timothy 3:1, 2 63
I Timothy 3:10 129
I Timothy 5:20 72
I Timothy 6:12 38
II Timothy 1:9 ....37, 38
II Timothy 2:3 73
II Timothy 2:10 38
II Timothy 4:2 72
II Timothy 4:13 61
II Timothy 4:18 37
Titus 1:2 ....37, 38
Titus 1:7 63
Titus 1:9 72
Titus 1:12 54
Titus 1:13 72
Titus 2:11, 12 18
Titus 2:13 33
Titus 2:14 52
Titus 2:15 72
Titus 3:7 38
Hebrews 1:8 37
Hebrews 1:9 124
Hebrews 2:6 ....49, 63
Hebrews 2:9 49
Hebrews 2:10 119
Hebrews 2:18 130
Hebrews 3:9 ....129, 130
Hebrews 4:15 130
Hebrews 5:6 37
Hebrews 5:9 ....38, 119
Hebrews 5:13, 14 114
Hebrews 6:1 118

Page

Hebrews 6:2 41
Hebrews 6:20 37
Hebrews 7:17 37
Hebrews 7:19 119
Hebrews 7:21 37
Hebrews 7:24 37
Hebrews 7:28 37
Hebrews 9:9 119
Hebrews 9:10 86
Hebrews 9:11 118
Hebrews 9:12 38
Hebrews 9:14 37
Hebrews 10:1 ....119, 120
Hebrews 10:14 ....119, 120
Hebrews 11:17, 37 ......130, 131
Hebrews 12:5 72
Hebrews 12:23 ....119, 120
Hebrews 13:5 25
Hebrews 13:8 37
Hebrews 13:20 37
Hebrews 13:21 37
James 1:2 131
James 1:4 118
James 1:12 131
James 1:13, 14 ....130, 131
James 1:17 118
James 1:25 118
James 1:27 63
James 2:9 72
James 2:19 120
James 2:22 120
James 3:2 118
James 3:6 45
James 5:14 123
I Peter 1:3 20
I Peter 1:7 129
I Peter 1:13 20
I Peter 1:18 52
I Peter 1:22 57
I Peter 2:1-3 107
I Peter 2:12 63
I Peter 2:19, 20 17
I Peter 2:25 63
I Peter 3:19, 20 47
I Peter 3:21 86

INDEX OF SCRIPTURE REFERENCES—Continued

	Page		Page
I Peter 4:11	37	Jude 6	47
I Peter 4:16	69	Jude 7	41
I Peter 5:10	37, 38	Jude 9	72
I Peter 5:11	37	Jude 13	41
II Peter 1:1	32	Jude 21	38
II Peter 1:3	75	Revelation 1:6, 18	37, 46
II Peter 1:4	82	Revelation 2:2, 3..72, 74, 128, 130
II Peter 1:11	32	Revelation 2:7	45
II Peter 2:1	51	Revelation 2:10	130
II Peter 2:4	47	Revelation 3:10	130
II Peter 2:17	41	Revelation 3:19	72
II Peter 2:20	32	Revelation 4:9, 10	37
II Peter 3:18	32, 37	Revelation 5:9	51
I John 1:1	48	Revelation 5:13	37
I John 1:2	38	Revelation 6:8	46
I John 1:3	111	Revelation 7:1-8	70
I John 1:8	82	Revelation 7:12	37
I John 2:5	121	Revelation 10:6	37
I John 2:20	124	Revelation 11:15	37
I John 2:25	38	Revelation 13:	70
I John 2:27	124	Revelation 14:9-11	42
I John 3:1	17	Revelation 15:7	37
I John 3:15	38	Revelation 19:20	44
I John 4:1	129	Revelation 20:10	40, 43
I John 4:12, 17, 18	118, 121	Revelation 20:13, 14	46
I John 5:11, 13, 20	38	Revelation 22:15	26
I John 5:21	69		